The NCTE Chalkface Series

Literary Terms: A Practical Glossary (1999), Brian Moon

Reading Hamlet (1999), Bronwyn Mellor

Studying Literature: New Approaches to Poetry and Fiction (2000), Brian Moon

Reading Stories: Activities and Texts for Critical Readings (2000), Bronwyn Mellor, Marnie O'Neill, and Annette Patterson

Reading Fictions: Applying Literary Theory to Short Stories (2000), Bronwyn Mellor, Annette Patterson, and Marnie O'Neill

Gendered Fictions (2000), Wayne Martino with Bronwyn Mellor

Investigating Texts: Analyzing Fiction and Nonfiction in High School (2001), Bronwyn Mellor and Annette Patterson

Studying Poetry: Activities, Resources, and Texts (2001), Brian Moon

Brian Moon
Literary Terms

A Practical Glossary

National Council of Teachers of English
1111 W. Kenyon Road, Urbana, Illinois 61801-1096

Staff Editor: Kurt Austin
Interior Design: Richard Maul
Cover Design: Diana Coe/ko Design Studio
Cover Photograph: ©Nola Lopez/Graphistock

NCTE Stock Number: 30089-3050

First published in Australia in 1992 by Chalkface Press P/L,
P. O. Box 23, Cottesloe, Western Australia 6011.

Library of Congress Cataloging-in-Publication Data
Moon, Brian.
    Literary terms: a practical glossary/Brian Moon.
        p. cm. — (The NCTE Chalkface series)
    Includes index.
    ISBN 0-8141-3008-9 (pbk.)
        1. Literature—Terminology. 2. English language—Terms and phrases.
    3. Literary form—Terminology. 4. Criticism—Terminology. I. Title.
    II. Series.

PN44.5 M57 1999
803—dc21
                                                    99-046413

Series Foreword

Twenty years ago we judged the success of our students' responses to a reading assignment by the similarity of their responses to a text with ours. We saw it as our job to help students read well, to read with understanding, to read correctly; in other words, we did our best to make students read as we read. We gave little thought to the processes and experiences at work that make a single reading of a text impossible and often even undesirable. We learn much, thank goodness, as we teach. By now we have learned to encourage our students to read diversely, to recognize the processes interplaying and influencing their readings, to examine the cultural factors influencing and the cultural consequences resulting from their reading practices.

Moving beyond encouragement to effective, integrated instruction and practice is always difficult. That is why we are so excited about the NCTE Chalkface Series. Never before have we seen such practical methods of examining and understanding the personal and cultural influences that affect students' reading. The lessons actively engage students and make the invisible processes of reading explicit, demystify responses to literature, and help students understand the myriad factors influencing their reading. These books, like no other secondary reading texts we have come across, had us seeking out colleagues to share our excitement about published lessons. We now do so at every opportunity.

Among the specific strengths in the books are the inclusion of theory and of questions that provide the basis for the applications/student practices. For example, in *Literary Terms: A Practical Glossary,* the study of each term is developed as a mini-lesson, including a short piece to help students with mind-set, a brief theoretical explanation, an activity that requires application, and a summary. Some terms are very common, such as *author* and *character;* others are less common, such as *polysemy* and *poststructuralism.* The material is student-accessible; the format is somewhat different from the traditional glossaries of literary terms. Students and teachers should find the activities very useful illustrations of the terms' definitions and the theories that serve as the foundations of the study of literature.

Gendered Fictions, another title in the series, operates essentially from the premise that texts offer differing "versions of reality" rather than a single illustration of the real world. The authors contend that we are conditioned to make sense of text by reading from a gendered position. They offer many opportunities for students to accept or challenge particular ways of looking at masculinity or femininity. A major question proposed by the text is *how* readers read—a critical question if we want our students to be analytical readers. Perhaps equally basic, the text encourages students to look at how they become what they become. As is true of the other books, the approach is not didactic. Questioning, yes; deterministic, no.

Reading Fictions follows similar assumptions: texts do not have a single, definitive meaning; rather, meaning depends on a number of variables. The authors do suggest that a text may very well have a *dominant* reading (i.e., what a majority of readers may agree is there), but it may also have *alternative* readings (i.e., what other readers may believe is there). The intent is to have students look at various texts and consider what may be a dominant reading or an alternative reading. Again, the intent is to facilitate skill, not to determine what students should believe.

Reading Hamlet positions *Hamlet* as a revenge tragedy and provides students with a context by offering a brief look at other revenge tragedies of roughly the same period: *Thyestes, Gorboduc, The Spanish Tragedy,* and *Titus Andronicus*. That may sound overwhelming; it is, rather, illustrative and offers a genuinely effective context for the study of *Hamlet*. The text also offers a number of ways for students to study character as well as opportunities for student performance. The performance component, in particular, gives students the opportunity to be actively involved with text. The author does not assume that students have to be talented actors.

Studying Poetry again offers opportunities for student performance, considerations of what poetry is, and exercise in writing critiques of poetry. Poems chosen for study range from traditional to contemporary. The book strongly encourages students to identify their own favorite poems, a practice also promoted by America's current poet laureate, Robert Pinsky.

Studying Literature goes to the fundamental question of what makes a piece of writing "literature," asking students to consider features of writing along with their own beliefs and values and encouraging them to reflect critically on the nature of the activity in which they are engaged rather than merely engaging in it.

Reading Stories lays a firm foundation for students moving toward becoming critical readers. From exploring their own expectations prior to reading a work (or rereading one) to questioning authorial intent to exploring cultural and social assumptions, this book makes explicit both the ways in which readings are constructed and the bases on which students might choose among them.

Investigating Texts builds on that foundation by exploring the deeper questions of how texts are made, how ways of reading change, and how texts can be read differently. As in all the books, numerous activities are provided to facilitate such exploration and application, promoting student interaction, an active relationship with the texts provided and, by extension, an active relationship with new texts they encounter.

We are delighted that NCTE has arranged to make Chalkface books available to its members. We are confident that teachers will share our enthusiasm for the publications.

Richard Luckert
Olathe East High School
Olathe, Kansas

William G. McBride
Colorado State University
Fort Collins

Contents

Acknowledgments   xii
Preface   xiii

Author   1
    Authorization   2
Binary Opposition   4
Character   9
Class   15
Code   19
    Character Code   20
    Suspense Code   20
    Plot Code   21
    Structural Code   21
    Cultural Code   21
Communication   24
Context   28
Conventions   33
    Reading Convention   34
    Textual Convention   34
Criticism   36
Culture and Nature   39
    Naturalization   40
Deconstruction   42
Denotation and Connotation   46
Discourse   50
    Dominant Discourse   51
    Alternative Discourse   51
    Oppositional Discourse 51
English Criticism   53
Feminist Criticism   57
    Patriarchy   57

Figurative Language	61
Simile	62
Metaphor	62
Metonym	62
Personification	62
Symbol	62
Foregrounding and Privileging	66
Gaps and Silences	70
Gender	74
Genre	78
Identification	82
Ideology	85
Imagery	88
Intertextuality	92
Allusion	93
Literature	96
Marxist Criticism	100
Narrative	103
Story	104
Plot	104
Omniscient Narrator	104
Limited Narrator	104
New Criticism	106
Point of View	110
Narrator	111
Third-Person Point of View	111
First-Person Point of View	111
Polysemy	114
Poststructuralism	118
Institution	119
Power	122
Hegemony	123
Psychoanalytic Criticism	126
Mirroring	127

Race   130
Reading Practices   134
   Resistant Reading Practice   135
Readings   138
   Preferred Reading   139
   Resistant Reading   139
   Alternative Reading   139
Representation   142
   Stereotypes   143
Semiotics   146
Structuralism   150
Style   155
   Diction   156
   Rhetorical Devices   156
   Sentence Organization   156
   Syntax   156
Text   160
   Closed Text   161
   Open Text   161
Theme   166
   Motif   167
Writing and Speech   170

Index   174
About the Author   177

Acknowledgments

Many thanks to Bronwyn Mellor, for invaluable help at all stages and for scrupulous editing; to Stephen Mellor for patient proofreading; and to Annette Moon for advice, support, and countless favors.

Texts referred to:

A Tale of Two Cities, Charles Dickens; *High Noon* (Dir. Fred Zinnemann); *Star Wars* (Dir. George Lucas); *Pride and Prejudice,* Jane Austen; *Sherlock Holmes,* Arthur Conan Doyle; *Hard Times,* Charles Dickens; *Pygmalion,* George Bernard Shaw; *S/Z,* Roland Barthes; *The Taming of the Shrew,* William Shakespeare; "Shall I Compare Thee to a Summer's Day?", William Shakespeare; *Nature's Way: Cooking Vegetarian,* Ellie Kantor; "The Beatles in Adelaide," Geoffrey Dutton; *Mark Welby, M.D.,* Lance Rylands; "Rapunzel," Traditional; "The Shell," Colin Thiele; *Heart of Darkness,* Joseph Conrad; *Sensations,* Western Australian Education Department; *Animal Farm,* George Orwell; "The Doll's House," Katherine Mansfield; *Twin Peaks* (Dir. David Lynch); "Little Red Riding Hood," Traditional; "The Company of Wolves," Angela Carter; *The Collector,* John Fowles; "A Birthday," Christina G. Rossetti; "The Love Song of J. Alfred Prufrock," T. S. Eliot; "The Rime of the Ancient Mariner," Samuel Taylor Coleridge; "The Highwayman," Alfred Noyes; "That Time of Year Thou May'st in Me Behold," William Shakespeare; *Jane Eyre,* Charlotte Brontë; *Wide Sargasso Sea,* Jean Rhys; *Peter Pan,* J. M. Barrie; *The Abyss* (Dir. James Cameron); *Macbeth,* William Shakespeare; *The Big Sleep,* Raymond Chandler; "Listen to the End," Tony Hunter; *Moby-Dick,* Herman Melville; "Cinderella," Traditional; "Jabberwocky," Lewis Carroll; "Theseus and the Minotaur," Traditional; "The Fall of the House of Usher"; Edgar Allan Poe; "Cat in the Rain," Ernest Hemingway; *School,* Lorelei Parker; "Ozymandias," P. B. Shelley; "A Christmas Tree and a Wedding," Fyodor Dostoyevsky; "Letters Never Mailed," James B. Hall; "The Secret Room," Alain Robbe-Grillet.

Preface

In recent years new theories including semiotics, structuralism, and poststructuralism have radically altered traditional approaches to English and literature study. Teachers and students now find themselves grappling with concepts as diverse and complex as deconstruction, ideology, representation, and resistant reading.

Literary Terms offers students and teachers a practical reference for this new literary terminology. Designed for use in high school and college courses, the book supplements traditional glossaries by focusing explicitly on emergent concepts and practices. It draws on a range of new developments in literary theory, placing special emphasis on the role of reading practices in the production of literary meanings. But the book also reviews many traditional terms, such as *character,* in the context of these new understandings.

Unlike traditional glossaries, *Literary Terms* takes a practical approach to its definitions. Terms are not only explained "in theory," but also demonstrated through brief activities using text extracts, puzzles, and problems to help students develop a working knowledge.

Each entry in the book is structured as a mini-lesson which provides:

a stimulating puzzle or problem that brings the concept into focus;
a brief theoretical discussion;
an activity which calls for practical application of the concept in textual analysis;
a final summary that can serve as a working definition of the concept.

Definitions and activities in the text are designed so that they can be used independently by students, at individual points of need. However, the glossary can also be integrated into classroom study without the need for additional preparation.

In keeping with its focus on contemporary approaches to literature study, the glossary is intentionally oriented toward concepts and issues rather than terms and "facts." It takes the view that literature is not a body of objective knowledge, but a field of social practice within which readers and writers act, and where meanings are negotiated and fought over. With this in mind, the glossary includes not only analytic terms, such as "point of view" and "imagery," but also brief accounts of some major critical orientations, such as structuralism, feminist criticism, and Marxist criticism. In acknowledging these differences within literary scholarship, the book aims to assist in the development of a democratic, active approach to the study of literary texts: an approach that will enable students to question the perspectives offered by the literary and critical texts they encounter—including this one.

Author

To get you thinking

■ Here is a list of different kinds of texts. Place a check next to those that you think have an author.

☐ A paperback novel   ☐ A science textbook
☐ A motion picture   ☐ A traditional fairy tale
☐ A TV news report   ☐ A theatrical performance
☐ A computer program   ☐ A recipe

■ What are the reasons for your decisions?
■ Use these ideas to make your own definition of *author* before reading on.

Theory

People commonly think of an author as an individual who produces an "original" work and who is the source of its meanings. But all texts have numerous indirect sources, and their meanings come not from individuals but from social practices, traditions, and institutions.

For example, a conventional novel is made up of:

■ a language shared by members of a culture;
■ a range of traditional literary conventions and techniques;
■ ideas adapted from the works of other writers;
■ formats and structures influenced by the needs of the publishing industry;
■ beliefs and values representative of specific groups in the culture;
■ and so on.

These raw materials already exist in the culture. They are not invented by any one person.

Because textual meaning is made possible by cultural systems such as language, and by the texts which have already been written and read, we need to challenge the idea that literary and other works are the product of individual genius. For this reason, many people now prefer the term *writer* to *author*. They think of a writer as someone who gathers raw materials from diverse sources and blends them together with reference to certain conventional rules.

We often see the concept of authorship used to give a text some kind of importance, or to "guarantee" its meanings by providing a point of origin. Wherever we see an individual, organization, or tradition used as the "guarantee" or source of a text's meanings, we see the process of *authorization* at work.

For example:

■ Fairy tales are authorized by "traditional wisdom." This creates the impression that culture is fundamentally unchanging, and that fairy-tale morals are always relevant and true (when in fact they may be racist, sexist, and thoroughly outdated).

■ Motion pictures are often authorized by the name of a famous director, scriptwriter, or actor. This creates the impression that the person concerned is responsible for the text, when in fact a film is the product of efforts by many people.

■ TV news is authorized by the supposed credibility of the presenter—even though she or he doesn't write the bulletins.

■ Literary texts are often authorized by a belief in the genius and originality of the writer. This ignores the fact that most texts use techniques and ideas drawn from the shared traditions and conventions of the culture, and that assessments of their value change over time.

In response to this kind of authorization we can ask:

■ Who or what is being promoted as the source of meaning for this text?

■ Who or what is creating this sense of authorship? Why?

■ What other sources of meaning are being denied?

■ What values or beliefs are being supported?

■ Who is being "empowered" by this action? Who is being "disempowered"?

Practice

Try writing down answers to the above questions for the following examples.

1. A teacher explains to his class what Shakespeare meant when he wrote his famous sonnet, "Shall I Compare Thee to a Summer's Day?" The teacher tells the students they will be questioned on this information in their next exam.
2. A publishing company launches the latest novel by the famous writer Nicholas Fudge. The advertising slogan reads, "The critics agree—Fudge is the most original writer of the decade, a stylistic genius. This is a unique book from a unique personality. Not since Shakespeare have we been blessed with a writer who can interpret life so clearly."
3. A television station promotes its newscasts by promoting the personality of its newsreaders. Its slogan is "Jack and Amanda and Channel 6—part of your family."

Summary

The author is the individual or group credited with writing a text. The term is often used to mean "originator" of a text, but modern theory argues that texts never have clear origins. There is now a preference for the term *writer*.

See also: text

Binary Opposition

To get you thinking

■ Fill in the blanks in this list with words or ideas that are commonly "opposed" to each other. Two examples have been done for you.

active / passive

_____ / low

male / _____

nature / _____

inside / outside

logical / _____

mind / _____

_____ / private

■ Why do most people find this such a simple activity?
■ Can you think of any word or idea that does not have a commonly accepted "opposite"?

Theory

Binary oppositions are words and concepts that a community of people generally regards as being "opposed" to each other. Oppositional thinking represents a "black and white" view of the world, a tendency to see everything in terms of simple contradictions. This is not a natural or innocent way of thinking. It has clear consequences for the way power is distributed among groups of people in a society. For example, the phrase "black and white," as used here, is not merely a convenient expression. It is also tied to divisive ideas about race which operate in our societies.

The binary opposition is an organizing principle for many texts and readings. The elements of a text are often structured around a pair of concepts such as _nature/culture, masculine/feminine, mind/body._ Through such oppositions, texts, and our ways of reading them, can embody and reproduce certain patterns of thinking.

One element in a binary opposition is often *privileged* over the other. This means that binary oppositions are also *hierarchies*, with one half dominating the other. The second term often comes to represent merely the absence of the first. This has the effect of devaluing the second element. Thus "emotion" is often degraded as merely the absence of "reason."

Binary patterns of thinking often mask the differences between things in this way, even though they seem to stress differences. This can be seen in the tendency to transfer concepts *between* binary pairs. For example, in the following list of oppositions, each *column* of terms may be read as belonging together in some way.

mind	body
masculine	feminine
rational	emotional
high	low

It is common, for example, for people to think of particular groups of people (such as men) as being rational, and of other groups (such as women) as being emotional. Through such connections, established patterns of thinking are supported, for it becomes difficult to change one set of terms without challenging an entire set of beliefs and practices. A study of binary oppositions in a text can reveal networks of links like those outlined above. Once identified, these can be traced to cultural assumptions which have been coded into the text.

For example, here is the opening chapter of Charles Dickens's novel, *A Tale of Two Cities*:

> It was the best of times, it was the worst of times, it was the age of wisdom, it was the age of foolishness, it was the epoch of belief, it was the epoch of incredulity, it was the season of Light, it was the season of Darkness, it was the spring of hope, it was the winter of despair, we had everything before us, we had nothing before us, we were all going direct to Heaven, we were all going the other way—in short, the period was so far like the present period, that some of its noisiest authorities insisted on its being received, for good or for evil, in the superlative degree of comparison only.

At first glance, this extract seems to compress many "opposites" into a short space. But by examining the pattern of oppositions we can show that the extract actually denies differences.

Here are some of the binary oppositions encoded in the text:

best	worst
wisdom	foolishness
light	darkness
spring	winter
hope	despair
belief	incredulity
Heaven	"the other way"

From these we can make some interesting suggestions:

■ Terms such as *light, hope, belief,* and *Heaven* suggest that this passage operates within the category of religious language (specifically, the Christian religion). Far from being diverse, the terms are all drawn from a common discourse, which implies a very specific way of thinking about the world.

■ This is confirmed when we read the columns vertically. The relationship that is established between *wisdom, belief,* and *Heaven,* for example, implies a rather narrow definition of "wisdom." (Can non-Christians be wise, according to this system?)

■ Perhaps most interestingly, the striking "oppositions" listed above are used to mask another common opposition: past/present. The text uses a string of "contrasts" to develop the argument that the past and present are essentially the same. The extract actually denies history, implying that human beings remain the same across time.

Practice

Many texts can be read in terms of structural oppositions, where aspects of storyline, character, or imagery can be decoded into binary forms. Here is a summary of the Western movie *High Noon,* which can be read in this way.

Sheriff Will Kane marries Amy, a pacifist Quaker. They plan to leave town and start a new life. But Kane hears that Frank Miller, an outlaw, and his gang are coming into town to seek revenge. The townsfolk and Amy urge Kane to leave while he can, but he believes it would be unmanly to run from danger. Amy does not accept Kane's decision to fight, and decides to leave the town and her new husband. Kane tries to organize a group of deputies to back him up, but no one will stand with him. They all advise him to leave. He visits the courthouse, the saloon, the church, his friends' homes, and even the former sheriff, in an effort to find support, but without success. One man is resentful that Kane did not recommend him for promotion; the former sheriff claims to be too old to fight; store owners argue that the Millers are good for business; the men in the church offer him moral support but will not fight. When the Miller gang rides into town, Kane must face them alone. In the midst of the gunfight, however, Amy returns from the train station, takes a gun from a man who has been shot, and helps Kane defeat the mob by shooting one of the Miller gang in the back. Afterward, Kane throws his sheriff's star into the dust, and he and Amy leave town.

1. Some of the oppositions suggested by this synopsis are:

lawman	outlaw
judicial law	the "law of the West"
man	woman
justice	injustice
willingness to fight	pacifism

As you can see, some oppositions represent contrasted ideas and concepts, rather than words or objects. Can you add other oppositions to the list?

2. Consider which elements in these oppositions are privileged by the classic Western story. (Consider, for example, that Amy must give up her beliefs, rather than Kane giving up his.) Circle the privileged elements on the list of oppositions.
3. What values or beliefs are implied by this privileging? Choose from among the following:

- [ ] Individualism
- [ ] Masculine "honor"
- [ ] Intellectual activity
- [ ] Physical activity
- [ ] Pacifism
- [ ] Communalism
- [ ] Confrontation
- [ ] Negotiation

Summary

Binary oppositions are structural features encoded in texts and reading practices. They are patterns of opposing concepts or ideas which work to reproduce a set of beliefs or values, and they serve particular interests.

See also: structuralism

Binary Opposition

Character

To get you thinking

List three of your favorite characters from novels, stories, movies, or TV programs you have encountered.

_____   _____   _____

■ For one of these characters, check the items in the following list which best explain why the character has significance for you. Add reasons if you wish.

☐ The character's personality appeals to you.

☐ You think you are like the character.

☐ You would like to be like the character.

☐ The character supports values you agree with.

☐ The character is a realistic representation of a "type" of person.

☐ The character is unusual or very different.

☐ The character meets requirements of the particular genre or text she or he is featured in.

Theory

Characters are constructed in texts and through our reading practices, from an assemblage of statements or descriptions. When descriptions of speech, action, and thought are referred to a proper name, we construct a reading of character from this information.

For example:

In this short extract, a set of statements is assembled around the name "Joan":

> Joan took her place in front of the class. She shuffled her feet. She placed her hands in her pockets, then behind her back, then in front. She cleared her throat, stared at the back wall, and began falteringly to speak.

We can construct from this information an imaginary "person." We can even infer that "Joan" is nervous—a piece of information not stated by the passage.

In the past, readers have often been encouraged to explore characters on a "personal" level. This means "getting to know" the characters by thinking of them as real people, and by sharing their experiences in an imaginary way. These traditional approaches to character study often make use of questions like these:

- What kind of person is Joan? Is she the sort of person you would like as a friend?
- Why does she behave in the way she does? Do you think she has good reason to act this way? How would you feel if you were in her position? Why?

This kind of questioning makes a number of assumptions about literary characters and about real people. It assumes that:

- people's actions are motivated from "within";
- individuals are wholly responsible for their own actions;
- individuals are unique and respond to situations in personal ways;
- we can (and should) judge people by comparing their thoughts with their actions;
- we can (and should) judge ourselves by comparing ourselves to others.

This approach sees characters as "morally accountable," in the same way that the popular beliefs, laws, and customs of Western society see real people as morally accountable. In other words, this approach to texts and characters supports a particular set of beliefs about people.

Reading a text in this way involves the reader comparing his or her "own" motivations and values to those of characters in the text. And in judging her or himself against the "people" in the text, the reader is also accepting and applying a particular set of beliefs about human nature and how people should act. In this way, the reader acts as her or his own "social conscience." The "personal" approach to reading becomes a way of training readers to learn and accept cultural values.

A problem with this approach to texts and characters is that it usually applies the same narrow set of values to everyone, for many of the characters and situations presented in "literary" texts have been produced within the values of powerful groups, often middle class, white, male readers and writers.

There are other ways of reading texts and the characters in them. One way is to examine the characters not as "real people" but as *signs* or *devices* which represent certain values in the text. For example, here are two "readings" of the character of fictional detective Sherlock Holmes.

> 1. Holmes has a rich and complex character. He is not only a great detective but a frustrated musician and a tireless campaigner for justice. His intellect is vast, and so we must forgive him for his impatience with those who cannot match his deductive skills. He is sympathetic to the plight of the common man, and he is not afraid to tackle authority head on if he feels that a wrongdoer is about to go unpunished. He is fearless in pursuing his enemies, loyal to his friends, and unswervingly committed to the triumph of good over evil. He is a deeply moral man; one we can all respect.
>
> 2. Sherlock Holmes is typical of a type of character which became common in literature in the nineteenth century. He represents the increasing influence of scientific rationalism in Western culture, and the replacement of organized religion by science as a way of explaining the world to people. As the all-seeing, all-knowing character who watches over the city and dispenses justice to wrongdoers, the Holmes character comforts readers with the idea that moral individualism would succeed where police forces and the law failed. He represents a middle/upper-class, masculine set of values—playing the violin, conducting arcane scientific experiments, and living an independent life free of the "responsibilities" of work, wife, and children.

These very different readings are produced in different ways and have different effects.

Reading 1 asks:

■ What kind of person is Holmes, and how do I, as a reader, respond to him?

One effect of this reading is that the reader comes to accept Holmes as a standard against which to judge her- or himself.

Reading 2 asks a different set of questions:

- ■ What function does this character serve in the text and culture?
- ■ What values and beliefs does the character support?
- ■ What readership is the character designed to appeal to?
- ■ How is the characterization produced?

One effect of this reading is to show that the values represented by the character are those of a particular group. This puts the reader in a better position to explore the way the text functions in the culture.

Practice

Here is one critic's brief reading of Elizabeth Bennet, a central character in Jane Austen's novel, *Pride and Prejudice*:

> Here at last is a heroine with a mind of her own! Robust, intelligent, and self-composed, Elizabeth refuses to passively submit to the conformity of her times. When there is no carriage to take her across the village, she walks, unconcerned that this is "unladylike" behavior. . . . Hers is an independent spirit. But she is not smug or self-centred. She is often more concerned for the welfare of others than for herself. Her greatest joy is seeing Jane happily reunited with Bingley; and she goes to great lengths to save her sister's reputation when Lydia elopes with Wickham. . . . Perhaps what makes her so likable, however, is her ability to make mistakes, and to admit them. She misjudges Darcy, as he misjudges her; but she is honest enough to see the error of her ways. Visiting his fine estate at Pemberley, she hears from his own servants what a good master Darcy is, and she sees the truth of Darcy's character revealed in the tastefulness and grandeur of his house. The prospect of being mistress of such a place—and such a man—delights Elizabeth. When she finally admits her love for Darcy, after having rejected him so thoroughly, the true strength of her character is revealed, and she finds her reward.

This extract is concerned to "reveal" Elizabeth Bennet's personality. But there is another way to read Elizabeth—that is, as a narrative device whose function is to endorse a particular set of beliefs about appropriate female behavior and ambitions.

1. Which of the following beliefs seem to be supported by the critic's description of Elizabeth Bennet above? Check your choices.

   ☐ Women and men should have equal opportunities—economically, educationally, industrially, and so on.

   ☐ Women should be dependent on men.

   ☐ Women should think of others rather than themselves.

   ☐ Women should have careers, interests, and expertise of their own.

   ☐ Every woman should want to find a husband.

   ☐ Being independent means being able to choose not to marry.

   ☐ A woman should guard against gaining a "reputation."

   ☐ Women should feel free to behave as men do in matters of sex.

2. On the basis of this evidence, how unique and independent is Elizabeth Bennet? Why might readers be encouraged to approach this novel—and other "romances"—through a personalized reading of character? What does such a reading obscure?

3. Romantic heroines such as Elizabeth Bennet, far from being unique and realistic, are constructed according to a rather narrow set of rules. Can you add to this list?

   The heroine should be:

   ■ lively and healthy;   ■ _____   ■ _____
   ■ sexually inexperienced;   ■ _____   ■ _____
   ■ moderately attractive;   ■ _____   ■ _____

4. What might be the corresponding rules for the romantic hero? Make a list of requirements for the hero.

5. Turn back to the notes you made earlier about a favorite character. Which method of character reading have you been trained to use—personal or "cultural-historical"?

6. Analyze one of your chosen characters using the four questions applied to Sherlock Holmes under the heading "Reading 2." Does this approach give you a different perspective on your character?

Summary

Characters are imaginary identities constructed through reports of appearance, action, speech, thought, and so on. Traditional reading practices assemble these reports to produce a "person." Modern practices explore characters as representing a set of beliefs and values. We can think therefore of character as an element of narrative "code."

See also: reading practices
resistant reading

Character

Class

To get you thinking

■ In column I below, rank the following from (1) highest to (10) lowest in terms of social class or status in your community.

	I	II	III
unpaid domestic worker			
business executive			
schoolteacher			
doctor			
factory worker			
lawyer			
secretary			
arts student			
farmer			
real estate agent			

■ In column II, rank the items as they would be ordered in a culture which regarded the care of the physical body as the most important thing in life.

■ In column III, rank the items as they would be ordered in a culture which regarded the pursuit of knowledge as the most important thing in life.

■ Look back now at your first ranking. What measures of respect and status did you apply? Why? What does this activity suggest about concepts of class?

Theory

In any society, different groups of people have different degrees of power and opportunity. This unequal distribution of power is the result of patterns of social organization. The concept of class is a way of categorizing groups of people on the basis of their birth, wealth, occupations, influence, values, and so on. Commonly used categories in Western societies are "working class," "middle class," and "upper class." Class divisions are always tied to the beliefs and values of a specific group of people; they are not natural and obvious. The class categories which prevail in a culture are those which reflect the interests of the most powerful group.

Economic class divisions were clear-cut in industrial Britain. The "upper class" consisted of those who inherited wealth and property. These people lived without the need to work. The "middle class" consisted of those who owned properties and businesses. The "working class" consisted of those who worked for wages in businesses they did not own. Class divisions are actually much more complex than these simple terms suggest, however. One person might have a great deal of influence in some situations and not others, or might hold values more commonly applied to another community group. And some groups of people might always have less power and influence in a community regardless of wealth or occupation.

In Western societies there is a strong belief that success or failure in life is determined by individual qualities rather than social circumstances. This belief in the individual draws attention away from unjust social conditions, and blames people for circumstances that are beyond their control. This is evident, for example, in the many texts that focus on characters with wealth and power. Such texts often invite readings that regard success as a matter merely of hard work. They tend to ignore the fact that many people's chances of obtaining wealth or power are limited by forces beyond their control. They also ignore the fact that other classes or groups might define success differently.

For example, in George Bernard Shaw's play, *Pygmalion*, a young woman who earns her living selling flowers on a street corner comes under the influence of a wealthy, aristocratic professor of linguistics. Professor Higgins sets about teaching Eliza Doolittle to speak and act like an upper-class lady. He makes a bet that he can pass Eliza off as a duchess at a garden party.

Here are some extracts from the play which make reference to Eliza's class background.

Higgins, chastising Eliza about her speech:

"A woman who utters such depressing and disgusting sounds has no right to be anywhere—no right to live. Remember . . . that your native language is the language of Shakespear and Milton and the Bible; and dont sit there crooning like a bilious pigeon."

Mrs Higgins, speaking to her son about Eliza:

"I dont think you realise what anything in the nature of brainwork means to a girl of her class."

Higgins, arguing with Eliza about her decision to leave him:

"Oh, it's a fine life, the life of the gutter. It's real: it's warm: it's violent: you can feel it through the thickest skin: you can taste it and smell it without any training or any work. Not like Science and Literature and Classical Music and Philosophy and Art. You find me cold, unfeeling, selfish, dont you? Very well: be off with you to the sort of people you like. . . . If you cant appreciate what youve got, youd better get what you can appreciate."

Readings of class invited by these extracts imply:

- that the language of the upper class is the "true" British language;
- that the working classes are less intelligent than upper classes;
- that the poor are insensitive and have no discrimination;
- that the poor have no philosophy or art or capacity for logical thought;
- that the poor should aspire to be like the rich in every way.

Practice

Here is an extract from *Hard Times* by Charles Dickens. It describes an industrial town in Victorian England.

It was a town of red brick, or of brick that would have been red if the smoke and ashes had allowed it; but as matters stood it was a town of unnatural red and black like the painted face of a savage. It was a town of machinery and tall chimneys . . . and vast piles of tall buildings full of windows. . . . It contained several large streets all very like one another, and many small streets still more like one another, inhabited by people equally like one another, who all went in and out at the same hours, with the same sound upon the pavements, to do the same work, and to whom every day was the same as yesterday and tomorrow, and every year the counterpart of the last and the next. These attributes of Coketown were in the main inseparable from the work by which it was sustained; against them were to be set off comforts of life which found their way all over the world, and elegancies of life which made we will not ask how much of the fine lady, who could scarcely bear to hear the place mentioned.

In this passage the nameless, anonymous workers are contrasted with the "fine lady" who cannot bear mention of the place.

1. Underline or circle in the passage words, phrases, or sentences which could be used to support the following class assumptions:

    ■ upper-class people cannot bear the thought of hard work;
    ■ working-class people have no individuality;
    ■ the ugliness of industrial towns merely reflects the dullness of their inhabitants;
    ■ the working classes are less civilized than the middle classes.

2. Are there any textual features in the passage to prevent such readings from being constructed?
3. What objections can you raise against such readings?

Summary

Class refers to a way of categorizing groups of people on the basis of their birth, wealth, occupations, influence, values, and so on. Class divisions always reflect the beliefs and values of specific groups of people; they are not natural and obvious.

See also: Marxist criticism

Class

Code

To get you thinking

■ Clothing and fashion constitute a social system which involves categories and rules. Complete this outline by adding further categories and rules to those listed.

Categories:

Bottoms	e.g., slacks, jeans, skirts
Accessories	e.g., belts, gloves, sunhats
_____	e.g., _____
_____	e.g., _____
_____	e.g., _____

Rules:

Wear only one item at a time from "bottoms" category.
Color is relevant when combining items.
Country of manufacture is not relevant when combining items.

_____
_____
_____
_____

■ Can you suggest possible categories and rules which are not part of the clothing and fashion system for your community? (For example: "Head to toe" coverings? Navel wear?)

Theory

Codes are systems of rules which enable us to make meanings with texts. These rules indicate how the elements in a text (for example, words, punctuation marks) should be combined in order to make sense to the members of a particular community. Codes are built up through social practices but also make such social practices possible, and impose limits on them.

When you get dressed in the morning, for example, your knowledge of the fashion code enables you to select and combine items from your wardrobe for the day's outfit. This combination of clothes is a "text" that other members of your community will be able to "read": it will tell them something about your mood, the activities you are planning to engage in, your social status, your sexuality, your financial position, and so on.

In order to produce "common" meanings through systems such as language, fashion, and gestures, members of a community must share a knowledge of the relevant codes. (In fact, we might say that sharing this knowledge is what makes people members of a community.) Unless both the "producer" and the "user" of a text adopt the same rules, they will make different meanings out of the same material. For example, if you are a member of an Indian community, you may not know how to "read" the traditional clothing of the Japanese. You may not know which items of clothing to wear on which occasion; you might not recognize the differences between women's and men's clothing.

Cultural differences can lead to conflicts over meaning. This arises because people who are located in different social "frameworks" may use a specific code in quite different ways. For example, in some cultures it is considered polite to look directly at someone who is talking to you, whereas in other cultures this is considered extremely rude. Both cultures have a "politeness code" (which might include gestures, forms of address, and so on) but their *uses* of the code differ. Similar situations can arise between groups within a culture, such as teenagers and adults, or different groups of teenagers.

Texts such as poems, novels, and films are assembled according to complex codes. Some of these are specific to "literary" or film texts, but codes such as fashion and gesture are also encoded in such texts.

The theorist Roland Barthes has suggested that *narrative texts* consist of five key codes:

- the **character code**: where descriptions of speech, appearance, etc., are grouped around a name (or object);
- the **suspense code**: techniques used to hold back information from the reader, with the intention of revealing all and tying it together at the end;

- the **plot code**: familiar patterns of story development drawn from other similar texts, which enable the reader to predict events;
- the **structural code**: techniques which structure the text around common oppositions such as good/evil, nature/culture, man/woman;
- the **cultural code**: general cultural knowledge (beliefs, values) which are drawn into the text from the culture which produced it.

According to Barthes, these basic codes are found in all narrative texts but may be used to produce different effects and types, or genres, of text. This means that mystery stories, for example, use the suspense code in one way, whereas romance stories use it in another.

Practice

Here is a brief extract from a Sherlock Holmes story. Read it a number of times. Then see if you can isolate the codes which are active in it, by completing the activity which follows.

> Hilton Cubitt was a tall, ruddy, clean-shaven gentleman whose clear eyes and florid cheeks told of a life led far from the fogs of Baker Street. He was a fine creature, this man of the English soil, simple, straight and gentle. His eyes rested upon the paper with the curious markings. "Well, Mr. Holmes, what do you make of this?" he cried.
>
> "It certainly is a curious production," said Holmes. "Why should you attribute any importance to so grotesque an object?"
>
> "I never should, but my wife does. It is frightening her to death. She says nothing, but I can see the terror in her eyes."

1. Number the following "pieces" of text to show which codes each one is located in. (Some pieces may relate to more than one code.) You may need to re-read the brief explanations of the codes to help you "classify" each of the "pieces" of text.

Item (a) has been completed for you as an example.

Codes
1. Code of **character**
2. Code of **suspense**
3. Code of **plot development**
4. Code of **textual structure**
5. Code of **cultural meanings**

Textual element	Code(s)	
Physical description of Hilton Cubitt	1	5
The absence of the terrified wife		
The use of formal terms of address ("Mr. Holmes")		
The linking of fog with Baker Street		
Holmes's complex vocabulary		
The reference to "English soil"		
The implied contrast between country and city		

2. Now try to explain the meanings produced by each of these uses of the story's codes. Here is an example which reads Holmes's complex vocabulary in terms of the codes of character and cultural meanings:

Through the *code of character:* Holmes's complex vocabulary indicates that Holmes is educated, and perhaps also suggests a keen analytical mind.

Through the *code of cultural meanings:* Holmes's complex vocabulary might indicate a belief in the benefits of education (of a particular kind), since Holmes is the story's hero.

Try explaining the linking of fog with Baker Street. Consider the cultural associations of fog and also how Baker Street represents both Holmes's residence and, more generally, the city. What meanings does this pairing activate?

Note: These meanings are not simply "in" the text. They depend very much on the codes available to readers in particular reading contexts. The fact that we can state the function of any piece of the text means that our training as readers makes it significant for us.

Summary

Codes are systems of rules which both enable and limit the meanings of textual elements. Although texts are produced in accordance with codes available to the writer, the codes that are available to readers also determine how the text is subsequently read.

See also: text

conventions

semiotics

Code

Communication

To get you thinking

■ One way of thinking about communication says that it is a process that involves a sender, a message, a medium, and a receiver. Try to fill in these categories for the examples below. (The first one has been done for you.)

Example	Sender	Message	Medium	Receiver
Romance novel	author	true love will prevail	written word	reader
TV commercial	————	————	————	————
Painting	————	————	————	————
Road sign	————	————	————	————

■ Problem: how does this model of communication account for the following possible outcomes?

☐ Receivers disagree with one another about the message.
☐ The message "received" is different from what was sent (e.g., readers make a different meaning to what an author "sent").
☐ A change of medium (e.g., when a novel is turned into a film) leads to different messages being received.

Theory

This model of communication (which we can call the "transmission model") assumes that a message is passed from a sender, through a medium, to a receiver, or "reader." It assumes that a message, or meaning, exists separately from other elements in the system, like a small child who is put onto a train by her parents, travels to another station, and is taken off by her grandmother.

But communication isn't so simple. For one thing, people often disagree about the meanings they obtain from texts; and for another, the same text seems to be read in different ways at different times and places. This model also ignores the fact that the received meaning may differ from one reader to another, according to differences in time, social position, cultural context, and so on.

Modern theories argue that communication is not about transporting meanings from one person to another but is a process in which meaning is constructed through the interaction between the text and a particular "reading framework." In this model, readers are not "receivers" who wait passively at the train station; they are users of particular "tools" of reading provided by the reading framework.

The reading frameworks within which readers operate are made up of many elements. These include the rules of a particular language, prevailing "common sense" ideas about life and about the function of reading, and specific ideas about textual conventions. Such rules are shaped by the social and historical contexts in which a reader is located. Because there are competing frameworks, which change over time, different readings can be produced of the "same" text.

This is clearly a more complicated idea of communication. It implies that the meanings being "communicated" within a culture are tied to complex—and often contradictory—social factors. We therefore need to replace the simple notion of "communication" with a more complex notion of *negotiated* or *contested meaning-production*. In modern usage this process is called *signification*: the use of social *signs* (such as words) to produce meaning.

Practice

Here is an extract from a tape-recorded job interview. The person conducting the interview is a middle-aged man in a senior position with a manufacturing company; the interviewee is a young woman. She is applying for a laboring job traditionally filled by male workers.

Manager: Come in Irene.
Applicant: Thank you, Mr Wiles.
Manager: (Checking files, then looking up) Well, you're certainly the prettiest of our applicants!
Applicant: (Seriously) I don't see how that relates to my application.
Manager: (Apologetic) I'm sorry, I didn't mean—it's just that most of the other applicants have been men, of course.

Applicant:	Why do you say "of course"? The ad said both men and women—
Manager:	Yes, that's right, you're quite right. You're certainly eligible to apply, no problem on that score. Now . . .(looks through files) . . . yes . . . your application doesn't say whether you have any children.
Applicant:	No, none.
Manager:	Any plans to?
Applicant:	Well, I haven't really—
Manager:	You see, the thing is, the last three fellows who had this job all left after just a couple of months, so we're looking for someone long-term, you know . . .

1. Consider the type of "framework" each of the speakers seems to be located within. Each speaker's language and behavior seems to be guided by different values and beliefs. Try to extend the following lists to include all the relevant factors.

Manager's "Framework"	Applicant's "Framework"
Company policies	Financial needs
Business factors	Career interests
Dominant gender assumptions	

2. Their location in different social "frameworks" leads the speakers to "read" the conversation in different ways. Consider the line spoken by the mananger: "Well, you're certainly the prettiest of our applicants! Which of the following are *possible* ways of reading this comment? (Check your choices)

   ☐ As an innocent attempt to break the ice by making humorous reference to the fact that most applicants have been men.

   ☐ As an attempt to stereotype the woman and trivialize her qualifications.

- ☐ As a piece of flattery suggesting that the manager finds the woman attractive, i.e., as a form of sexual harassment.
- ☐ As a compliment intended to boost the applicant's confidence.
- ☐ As a demonstration of the unequal power relationship in the interview, which enables the manager to make personal comments.

3. Which readings has the manager apparently produced?
4. Which readings has the applicant apparently produced?

Note: This is not merely a personal difference; it is a difference between two systems of belief and action which have real effects on people's lives.

5. Choose two other statements from the text where the meaning has been or could be "contested" by the participants, and underline them. Then list some possible readings of the statements.

To think about: How much choice do readers have in determining the reading practices they use? How does this choice come about? (For example, can the man simply "choose" to change his language and behavior? Why/why not?)

Summary

Communication is not a transmission of meaning. It involves the negotiation or contesting of meanings from particular social frameworks. Modern approaches to language and literature prefer the term *signification*.

See also: reading
         ideology
         discourse

Communication

Context

To get you thinking

■ Imagine yourself taking an exam in which you have been asked to analyze a Shakespearean sonnet. Below is a list of factors which might shape the reading you produce. Some factors might shape the reading in a very direct way; others might have an indirect influence. Number the items from 1 (most direct) to 10 (least direct/not available).

Influence	Number
Your culture's perceptions of Shakespeare	
Your training in critical analysis	
Your "personal" experiences and values	
Shakespeare's "personal" reasons for writing the sonnet	
The dominant values and beliefs of your society	
The politics and literary values of Elizabethan England	
The "original" (17th century) meaning of the words	
Changes in word meanings since the poem was written	
The structure and workings of the modern education system	
The exact wording of the exam question	

■ Does this suggest that the reading will be most powerfully shaped by "present day" factors, or by "historic" factors?
■ Do you think it is possible for you to produce the same reading that might have been produced by a reader in Elizabethan England? Why/why not?

Theory

Context has often been thought of as the "social background" of a text and its writer—a source of "extra" information about the text. Critical methods which employ this idea claim that finding out about the "life and times" of the writer and text can lead to a more accurate interpretation of the text's meaning. This approach has a number of problems, however.

The first problem is that knowledge of the "social context" is never available in a pure form. To take the example of Shakespeare, there is no one living who can offer a firsthand report of Elizabethan England. We have to rely on recorded histories, which are often incomplete, and which present the material from a particular position. That is to say, the histories we have available to us are *readings* of the past, rather than objective, "true" accounts.

The second problem is that any society is a mixture of competing beliefs, values, and ways of acting. This means there is no "single" context to refer to anyway. It is therefore difficult to generalize our information. "People in Shakespeare's day really believed in witches and ghosts, so they would have read the plays differently from us": this is a common generalization. But some people in the twentieth century certainly *do* believe in witches, and some Elizabethans certainly *did not*. Whose "context" do we refer to?

Finally, because readings are produced by the interaction of textual factors and *ways of reading* that prevail in a given time and place, the meaning of a text cannot be said to lie in the past. Rather, the text is a site on which many meanings are built in the course of history, some of which may openly contradict one another. Thus the text's "context" is always shifting, never stable.

For all these reasons, the traditional idea of context must be broadened. We can say that context refers to the multitude of factors which shape the meanings of a text within the social framework of its *reading*. This framework may include particular ideas about the text's history, but it is also powerfully shaped by competing beliefs and practices in the present.

Practice

Shakespeare's play *The Taming of the Shrew,* written around 1623, concerns in part the courtship and "taming" of Katharine, a "shrewish woman," by Petruchio. Much of the play focuses on Petruchio's efforts to discipline Katharine by alternately praising and berating her. He finally transforms her, and at the end of the play calls upon Katharine to offer advice about how a woman should look upon her husband.

Here is some of what she has to say:

> Thy husband is thy lord, thy life, thy keeper,
> Thy head, thy sovereign; one that cares for thee . . .
> Such duty as the subject owes a prince,
> Even such a woman oweth to her husband . . .

If we think of context merely as the historical background of a text, we might explain this play with the following details:

- People in Elizabethan times believed that the world had a "natural" order set up by God, in which angels were higher than sovereigns, sovereigns were higher than men, men were higher than women, women were higher than animals, and so on.
- Stories about the taming of shrewish women had a long history in the culture, and Shakespeare's play makes use of this material.
- Therefore, the play must be read within the tradition of stories about maintaining a natural order in the world.

This approach suggests that the play's meaning is grounded in the past, and it uses a particular construction or version of past beliefs to excuse aspects of the text which are now read as objectionable.

1. For modern readers the play is located within an area of important social debate. The following are some of the "issues" which might be active in shaping modern readings of the play. Rank them according to the likely strength of their influence.

Issue	Rank
Men and "masculinity"	
Women and "femininity"	
The institution of marriage	
Domestic violence	
The relation between "public" and "private" aspects of life	

Might these issues have framed Elizabethan readings also? (Do we have any records of how women viewed men "disciplining" them?)

2. This second list, below, refers to practices of reading which might influence your approach to the text. Rank them from most relevant (1) to least relevant (7).

Reading Practice	Rank
Reading characters through their "psychology"	
Reading for "traditional" elements	
Reading for realism and "believability"	
Reading for "social comment"	
Reading for beautiful language	
Reading for cleverness of language (e.g., puns)	
Reading Shakespeare as "Serious Literature"	

What other factors might shape the modern "reading context" for Shakespeare's play?

Summary

Context refers to the multitude of factors which shape the meanings of a text within the social framework of its reading. This framework may include particular ideas about the text's history, but it is also powerfully shaped by competing beliefs and practices in the present.

See also: intertextuality

Context

Conventions

To get you thinking

■ Which of the following are features of a typical "Western" movie? (Place a check next to your selections.)

Characters and Story:

☐ The sheriff is a loner.
☐ The outlaw is the leader of a gang.
☐ The schoolteacher is a man.
☐ The man who runs the store comes from outer space.
☐ The shoot-out occurs in the middle of the film.
☐ Justice is defeated in the end.

Presentation:

☐ The story is punctuated by song and dance routines.
☐ The actors sometimes play characters of a different sex.
☐ Time changes are indicated by fading out and fading in.
☐ Scene changes are signalled by raising and lowering a curtain.
☐ Events are presented in chronological order.

Theory

The items which you have checked in this activity are conventions. These are common features of texts and readings which help to stabilize the range of meanings that circulate in a society.

Texts do not simply "reflect" the real world. Instead, they produce *versions* of reality by organizing their elements according to certain familiar rules or *codes*. Similar codes guide the *reading* of texts and determine which features will be considered significant. If textual codes and reading codes did not match up, or if too wide a range of codes was available, the number of competing readings of any text would be so great as to be confusing. By applying the rules in repetitious ways, texts and reading practices reduce the degree of confusion through familiar patterns and methods. They enable stories to get told, for example, without *everything* having to be explained.

Because so many of the texts which circulate in a culture work in similar ways, the process of reading seems obvious or natural. But ways of reading are highly *conventional*. Changes in reading practices may only become apparent over long periods of time, or in very different cultures. It has been suggested that readers in the seventeenth century did not think of the characters in stories as "individual people" but merely as "conventional types," like the pieces on a chess board. Modern reading practices, however, read characters in terms of their "psychology"—from the inside rather than the outside. *Both* ways of readings are conventional.

It can be useful sometimes to distinguish between *textual* conventions and *reading* conventions, even though the two are not always separate. Examples of textual conventions would be: the use of a musical soundtrack on films; the division of plays into scenes; the division of novels into chapters; the use of an a-a-b-b-a rhyme scheme in limericks. Examples of reading conventions would be: reading characters through "psychology"; looking for a theme in a text; reading "silently" (this too is a recent development).

Practice

Here is a famous sonnet by William Shakespeare. Read the poem; then work through the activity below.

Shall I compare thee to a summer's day?
Thou art more lovely and more temperate:
Rough winds do shake the darling buds of May,
And summer's lease hath all too short a date:
Sometimes too hot the eye of heaven shines,
And often is his gold complexion dimmed,
And every fair from fair sometime declines,
By chance, or nature's changing course untrimmed;
But thy eternal summer shall not fade,
Nor lose possession of that fair thou ow'st,
Nor shall Death brag thou wandrest in his shade,
When in eternal lines to time thou grow'st
So long as men breathe or eyes can see,
So long lives this, and this gives life to thee.

Through this poem we can explore the two types of conventions. Use T, R, or B to indicate whether each of the following is a "textual" or "reading" convention, or "both" (sometimes it can be hard to tell).

Convention	Type
Sonnets have fourteen lines.	
The speaker is a man, addressing a woman.	
The poem makes use of comparison.	
Sonnets are about "love."	
Rhyme scheme is abab-cdcd-efef-gg.	
The comparisons are drawn from nature.	

Summary

Conventions are common uses of textual or reading codes which stabilize the range of meanings which may be applied to a text.

See also: code
          genre
          reading practices

Conventions

Criticism

To get you thinking

■ Here are three readers' responses to a novel. For each one, try to describe what each reader looks for or values in a novel. (The following checklist may be helpful: stylistic devices, personal relevance, narrative construction, structure, realism, coherence, originality, credibility, insightfulness, relevance to life, engagement with social issues, consistent characterization.)

I really loved it. The main character reminded me so much of my best friend—she has the same sense of humor. Also, the things that happened remind me of what I used to get up to while I was young.

Focus:

This is the most successful of the author's three novels. The characterization is much more consistent than in the previous books, and the use of first person point of view draws the reader into the events. But best of all, there is a strong moral to the story.

Focus:

The most interesting feature of this work is the way it is structured around oppositions between male and female, good and bad. These four categories work as a grid within which every character's position can be mapped, and this grid then functions to organize all of the other elements in the narrative—especially the setting.

Focus:

Theory

The term *criticism* comes from the Greek word *kritikos*, a judge, and so it implies the formation of judgments about a text. Of the three examples above, only the second would normally be labelled "criticism." The first would be called a "personal" response, and the last might be called a structural analysis. But the differences between them are not as clear as they might seem, for each one implies a theory about how texts work, what their purposes are, and how they can be classified.

Different criticisms are defined by the assumptions they work from and by the elements they focus on. Some forms of criticism assume that texts "reflect" real life; others argue that texts produce imaginary worlds which relate to social reality in very complex, mediated ways. Some criticisms aim to judge works as either good or bad; others aim to demonstrate how a text works.

Criticism is not a "scientific" practice: there are no universal laws or truths which can be applied to the study of texts. Instead of such laws, criticisms establish their own criteria for analyzing or judging a text. These criteria reflect the beliefs and values of different cultural groups and different historical periods. The ancient Greek philosopher, Plato, for example, argued that all poetry should be banned because it offered people *images* of reality rather than a *true experience* of reality. In contrast, the American New Critics of the 1930s argued that poetry was the highest expression of reality.

If criticism cannot offer absolute truths, it can nevertheless have powerful moral and political *effects*. Traditional English criticism, for example, argued that literary texts contained universal truths and represented the voice of all humanity. In contrast, modern feminist criticism successfully argues that the language and texts of our culture silence the contributions and experiences of women. Like all social practices, therefore, criticism involves a struggle for meanings and power between different sets of beliefs and practices.

Practice

Different critical methods are characterized by different assumptions—about texts, reading, reality, and so on. Refer back to the critics' responses at the start of this entry, and next to each statement below, record the number(s) of the response(s) which seem to match it.

Statements	Number(s)
Literature is a reflection of life.	
Literature should aim to instruct us.	
Literary texts are complex, self-enclosed structures.	
Literature should provoke a personal response.	
Literature should be judged by "objective" criteria.	
Literary texts contain messages.	
Literary texts have universal messages.	

Which of these statements best seem to sum up the critical methods you have learned?

Summary

Criticism is a systematic way of reading and talking about texts. Critics analyze and evaluate texts according to methods made available to them by their location within a framework of beliefs and practices.

See also: English criticism
structuralism
New Criticism
Marxist criticism
poststructuralism
psychoanalytic criticism
feminist criticism

Criticism

Culture and Nature

To get you thinking

■ In the spaces provided, try to give the meaning of "culture" for each of the following sentences.

I go to the opera whenever I feel the need for some culture.
Culture = _____
Personality is influenced more by culture than by nature.
Culture = _____
The new drug is extracted from a bacterial culture.
Culture = _____

■ Which meaning seems most often applied to a study of literary texts?

Theory

The meaning of the term *culture* varies enormously according to the context in which it is used. In popular usage, culture often refers to activities and beliefs which are considered refined, and civilized. This is the meaning in the first sentence, above.

For our purposes, culture refers to the social relations, practices, beliefs, and values which prevail in a community of people. These relations are established through basic human activities such as language use, kinship systems, and practices for producing the necessities of life. Human beings are separated from nature in a way that no other species is. Where most creatures must live within natural limits, human beings can manipulate nature in such a way that these limits no longer apply. We can see an example of this process in human reproduction: producing offspring is a matter of choice for human beings in a way that is not true for animals.

Humans have the capacity to live their lives in a variety of ways. However, societies do not usually exploit all of the possibilities. Instead, a particular pattern of living is usually promoted. Through the process of *naturalization*, this pattern is presented as the most "natural," and therefore the most sensible. For example, we see many stories in which women who initially choose not to have children finally see the error of their ways and find fulfillment in having a family. In this way, literary texts work to "naturalize" certain ways of living. This always works in favor of some groups in the culture, and at the expense of others.

Cultures are not unified wholes, therefore. Although people may share many social practices, including a language, they may not all have equal status or power. A shared language may be used to divide people as well as to unify them. In the study of literary texts we can often see these processes of division and oppression. The beliefs and values which a text supports, often by claiming them to be "natural," will work in favor of some groups and against others. As cultural artifacts, texts of all kinds function as weapons in the ongoing struggles for power between groups of people. This can be seen most clearly in the disputed meanings of texts such as the Bible or the Koran, but it is also evident in critical debates over Shakespeare or Harlequin romances.

Practice

Here is an extract from a popular vegetarian cookbook called *Nature's Way*.

We all have a natural desire for variety and color in our meals. Follow the recipes in this section and you'll produce dishes to tempt the eye as well as the palate of your friends. Use the photographs as a guide for presentation. Remember that a meal should be a social occasion. Use bold napkins or colorful serving dishes for a dramatic touch. And don't forget to top it off with a good wine!

1. The book promotes a "natural" approach to meals. Which of the following would you agree are "natural"? (Check your choices.)

☐ Needing to eat   ☐ Wanting colorful meals
☐ Using crockery   ☐ Eating cooked food
☐ Drinking wine   ☐ Needing a variety of foods
☐ Eating "socially"   ☐ Choosing a vegetarian diet

2. Is this "natural" way of eating available to everyone? How might the following factors affect someone's ability to follow this advice?

    ☐ Financial considerations?
    ☐ Mobility? (e.g., consider people with disabilities)
    ☐ Time?
    ☐ Cultural beliefs? (regarding wine, meat, etc.)

3. What can you conclude from these activities:

    ☐ The cookbook presents a natural alternative?
    ☐ The cookbook is merely naturalizing a specific cultural practice?

Summary

Culture refers to the beliefs, values, practices, and products through which human beings construct their relationships with themselves, with the natural world and with each other. These elements of culture provide the context for a study of literary texts.

See also: representation
         ideology
         discourse

Culture
and Nature

Deconstruction

To get you thinking

■ How many readings can you make of each of the following statements? How many meanings can each one have?

Children must be carried on escalators.
All refuse to be put in this basket.
Our grannies reduced this week. (Fruit store sign)
Swim between the flags.

■ How do so many people make the "right" meaning from such signs?

Theory

Traditional approaches to literary texts have assumed that meaning is located "in" a text, and that texts offer a narrow range of meanings to readers. They assume that meanings are relatively stable. In contrast, the simple examples above show that meaning can be very "slippery."

As cultural products, texts are crafted from the competing beliefs, values, and ways of speaking of a particular society at a particular time. This means that texts are assembled from contradictory elements, just as a patchwork quilt is assembled from materials of different colors and shapes. But our reading and writing practices try to downplay the contradictory nature of texts. Deconstruction is a critical practice which focuses on contradictions and slippages of meaning in order to remind us that the meanings we make when we read are neither obvious nor neutral. It suggests that meanings are "pinned down" or stabilized not by language, but by the force of dominant cultural beliefs.

For example, suppose you come across these lines in a novel:

When all is said and done, Marlow was a real character. Funny, direct, sly. There was something about him that drew folks in, made them want to get to know him. He was one of those people you wanted to have for a friend.

In a conventional novel, we might read these lines as a technique for bringing Marlow "to life." A deconstructive reader might challenge this idea, however, perhaps by focusing on the contradictions in a phrase such as "a *real* character." This reader might point out that "character" can mean:

- a person's "personality";
- a fictional person;
- a typographical letter;
- a quality;
- an actor's role.

A deconstructive approach would argue that readers must "ignore" some of these meanings in order to produce the dominant reading of the text, which constructs Marlow as a "real" personality. Based on many of the above meanings, "real character" would seem to indicate "a make-believe" person. So readers must "forget" that the character is a fictional construction.

Deconstruction does not point out such contradictions in order to "destroy" texts, but to improve our reading of them. It argues that texts are always read in terms of particular beliefs and values, which smooth over contradictions in order to make particular ways of life seem natural. In the above example, a powerful belief in the uniqueness of individuals smooths over the contradiction between character as a *construction* and character as a quality that emerges *from within*. This approach shows how the reading of literature can promote some values over others.

This glossary makes use of many deconstructive terms and concepts.

Practice

Here is the opening paragraph of Jane Austen's novel, *Pride and Prejudice*:

It is a truth universally acknowledged, that a single man in possession of a good fortune, must be in want of a wife. However little known the feelings or views of such a man may be on his first entering a neighborhood, this truth is so well fixed in the minds of surrounding families, that he is considered the rightful property of some one of their daughters.

1. Here is one possible way of reading the first sentence. Try to add to the list. (You might find it useful to read the lines as sincere; then as ironic; then as sarcastic, etc.)

    ☐ The narrator is stating his or her own belief.
    ☐
    ☐

2. Try to construct arguments to show that the text supports each of the following readings.

    ☐ It is a fact that wealthy men want wives.
    ☐ Only foolish people think wealthy men want wives.
    ☐ Everyone believes that wealthy men want wives, but it may not be so.

    Is it possible to say which reading is "correct"? (Note: some people will say that the meaning can only be clarified by comparing it to other sections in the text. But if we look closely, we find that those "other parts of the text" are equally difficult to pin down!)

3. Is there a reading you would want to promote as better than other readings? Why? On what bases?

4. Here are some beliefs which might underlie certain readings of the text.

    ☐ Men need wives more than women need husbands.
    ☐ Women need husbands more than men need wives.
    ☐ Popular wisdom is not to be trusted.
    ☐ Popular wisdom is the best measure of truth.
    ☐ Daughters are less valuable to a family than sons.
    ☐ Sons are less valuable to a family than daughters.

    What beliefs would your preferred reading be based on?

Summary

Deconstruction is a form of criticism which argues that texts can support multiple readings, many of which are contradictory. It demonstrates that a preference for one reading over another is always based on certain beliefs and values, and is not guaranteed by "the words on the page."

See also: poststructuralism

Deconstruction

Denotation and Connotation

To get you thinking

■ What associations do the following words commonly have in your culture? Follow the example and record your responses.

Home: safety   rest   privacy   support

Rose:

Father:

Money:

Clouds:

■ Where do these associations come from? Are they "in the word," or somewhere else? And are they the same for everyone?

Theory

Many of the words we use seem to have two "levels" of meaning: a basic, dictionary type meaning, and a set of associations like the ones you have listed above. These are commonly called denotative and connotative meanings. *Denotation* is said to be the literal or "factual" meaning; *connotation* is said to be the suggested or implied meaning. For example, it is generally agreed that "rose" denotes a type of plant; but the connotations of the word might include: *love, romance, fragility,* and so on.

  These meanings are not contained in the word, of course. They are attached to the word by social usage and by the contexts within which it is read. This means that people located within different "reading frameworks" might produce different denotative and connotative meanings for the "same" word.

For example, here are two possible readings of the word *police*.

1. **Denotation**: government workers who uphold justice and the law.
   Connotation: protection, security, order.
2. **Denotation**: government workers who maintain social inequality.
   Connotation: harassment, repression, danger.

What kind of reading framework might each of these readings come from? Would reading 2 only be produced by "criminals," or might it also be produced by readers located in other reading contexts; for example, where prevailing laws do not recognize their rights?

Some approaches in the study of literature emphasize connotation as the key to a text's meaning. This applies especially to the study of poetry. We need to recognize that these approaches do not "uncover" a meaning buried in the poem. Rather, they construct a reading of the poem that seems correct or desirable from within specific reading contexts. This doesn't mean that we can ignore the distinctions constructed between denotation and connotation. It means that we must become aware of how these concepts operate to make certain readings seem "natural" and obvious.

Practice

This is the opening stanza of a poem, "The Beatles in Adelaide," by Geoffrey Dutton:

> Give way, square city named for a dull dead queen,
> Bulge like the trousered bottoms of squealing sixteen.
> Sag like their sweaters, elegant old verandah
> Of the hotel where Schnabel or Menuhin once were seen
> And whispered on by black-tied and jewelled guests at dinner.

(Background information: The Beatles were a controversial pop group in the 1960s, popular with the young, but viewed with suspicion by many older, more conservative people. Adelaide is the capital city of South Australia. In the 1960s it was well known for "serious" arts. Schnabel and Menuhin are names of classical musicians.)

1. Can you give denotative ("dictionary") meanings for the following words from the poem?

   ☐ square: a geometric shape with four sides of equal length, joined at right angles;
   ☐ sixteen:
   ☐ black-tie:
   ☐ Schnabel and Menuhin:

2. Here are two ways of reading this stanza of the poem. What reading "framework" or context might each emerge from? (Consider the values, beliefs, and activities which might inform each reading.)

   A. The poem celebrates the arrival of modern music in a very conservative city. It conveys the feeling of excitement that the Beatles' tour produced.
   B. The poem defends traditional values by mocking the new fashions. It expresses nostalgia for "serious" music.

3. List the "associations" or connotative meanings of the same words in terms of these two readings of the poem.

	Reading A	Reading B
square:	old fashioned, dull	
sixteen:		
black-tie:		
Schnabel/ Menuhin:		

Would these two readings be in complete agreement about the denotative meaning also? How might arguments about denotation and connotation be used to support one or another of these readings?

4. Does your list of denotations seem completely neutral and obvious?

Summary

Denotation and connotation distinguish between the "literal" and "associative" meanings of a word or phrase. However, these distinctions are always produced and maintained within specific reading frameworks. They do not hold true for all readings of a text.

See also: figurative language

Denotation and
Connotation

Discourse

To get you thinking

■ Here are some categories of language that are used in our culture. For each one, write down who is qualified to speak this language, who it will be spoken to, where it will be spoken, and what objects will be spoken about.

Medical language

Speaker: _____ Hearer: _____
Place: _____ Object: _____

Legal language

Speaker: _____ Hearer: _____
Place: _____ Object: _____

Literary language

Speaker: _____ Hearer: _____
Place: _____ Object: _____

Religious language

Speaker: _____ Hearer: _____
Place: _____ Object: _____

■ In each case, who is made "powerful" by the language? How? Who is made "powerless"?

Theory

All areas of human activity have their own "languages," which include not only terms and concepts but also ways of speaking. These categories of language are called *discourses*. They operate according to unwritten rules about who can speak, who is spoken to, and what kinds of things can be talked about. They also operate according to certain relations of power, as the examples above show.

Discourses do not offer neutral descriptions of the world. They actively shape the world in favor of certain viewpoints. They also compete with one another for control of certain aspects of life. Wherever we find one discourse, we know that it is taking the place of another which could be there. For example, what Western cultures now call "mental illness" was once regarded as "possession." This change in thinking has been due in part to the fact that madness has become a subject of medical discourse rather than a subject of religious discourse. In simple terms, this might show a movement of power from priests to doctors.

Discourses which operate from positions of power are known as *dominant* discourses. Those which seek to operate from other positions are *alternative* or *oppositional* discourses. Literary texts always bear traces of many different and competing discourses, but in the processes of reading and writing, dominant discourses tend to obscure alternative and oppositional forms. In this way, texts and readings *privilege* some views of the world over others, and basic contradictions are hidden. By teasing out the discourses of a text, and observing which ones seem to be privileged, we can find out which views a text supports.

Practice

Read this brief extract from the opening of a popular novel.

Northside Hospital was a sprawling, glittering marvel spread over three hectares, with a central administration block of steel and glass that flung itself triumphantly twelve stories up into a cloudless sky. A decade in construction, not counting the three-month delay while protesters lay in the mud in front of the bulldozers, the complex catered for half the city's medical needs, with unheard of efficiency. It was, simply, the best hospital in the state. And I, Mark Welby thought to himself, am part of it!

Striding across the busy reception hall after completing his rounds in Cardiac, the young Dr. Welby collided with Nurse Sally Mitchell, a green-eyed blond whose willowy frame had caught his attention from day one. He caught her before she fell, and slipped his arm around her waist protectively. "Sorry Sally, are you okay?" he inquired. "I'm fine Dr. Welby, I just wasn't looking where I was going." She blushed at the sudden closeness, then straightened her cap and skirt.

"Well, I'm glad it was you I bumped into and not Sister Greer," he joked, thinking of the stern woman who ran the wards in C Block. "She would have seen it as a political act, I'm sure!"

1. Here are some of the discourses which dominate the writing in this passage. Mark out some examples in the texts as follows:

   ☐ the discourse of "progress" (underline);
   ☐ medical/professional discourse (dotted underline);
   ☐ romantic/sexist discourse (double underline);
   ☐ discourses of power—for example, forms of address (circle).

2. The passage shows how the dominant discourses of medicine, progress, gender, and power "fit together" in our culture. These discourses work in opposition to others which have been marginalized or silenced. Re-read the passage and identify traces of these absent discourses. That is, look for fragments or references to:

   ☐ environmental or conservation discourse (circle these);
   ☐ feminist or anti-sexist discourse (use square brackets).

3. What issues are suggested by this pattern of discourses? (For example, "romance" versus "sexual equality"?) What position does this text take on these issues?

4. Which of the following interest groups are served by the ways of thinking, acting, and speaking supported by this passage?

   ☐ professional men   ☐ professional women
   ☐ feminists   ☐ male chauvinists
   ☐ developers   ☐ conservationists
   ☐ mainstream medicine   ☐ alternative medicine

Summary

A discourse is a category of language which relates to particular social practices. Discourses shape the attitudes, behaviors, and power relations of the people involved.

See also: ideology

Discourse

English Criticism

To get you thinking

■ Imagine that you have been given ten novels to read, and that you have been asked to judge their quality. List some of the factors you would consider in this task.

realism?   moral values?

■ Which of these factors might cause the most arguments among readers?

Theory

English Criticism is a term applied to the kind of literary analysis practised by F. R. Leavis and Q. D. Leavis, who edited a journal called *Scrutiny* in 1932. Their method emphasized that the goal of literary analysis was to judge the *value* of a piece of writing. They assumed that genuine literary works should express the highest human values and ideals.

In many respects, this view of literature study was almost religious. It created the impression that the study of "great works" *improved* people, both intellectually and morally, because such texts put the reader in touch with the wisdom of "great minds." More recent theories have challenged English criticism on a number of points, including its focus on the author, its view of language, and its values.

English Criticism saw the text as an *expression* of the author's thoughts and feelings about life. It assumed that texts were like transparent containers into which preexisting thoughts and feelings could be placed. A literary work was judged in part according to how well it preserved the author's *intention* (that is, whether it was a worthy and effective container for the author's meaning).

Modern literary theory has overturned these ideas by demonstrating that language and texts are not containers for meaning: they are structures with which readers *make* meaning. In modern practice, the goal is not to find the author's meaning in the text, but to explore the meanings given to a text by specific groups of readers.

English Criticism's ideas about value have also been challenged. Different groups of people live by different values, and reading/writing practices reflect these differences. This means that there are no universal values which can be used to judge a text: judgments are always related to the specific values of the people who do the judging. The list of great works established by the Leavises, and the methods they used, reflect the beliefs and values of middle-class, white, educated people of 1930s Britain. They are not "objective" judgments.

This form of criticism also failed to realize that literary judgments are shaped in part by social practices, and by the economic organization of a culture. For example: until the nineteenth century, publishing companies were unwilling to publish works by women. As most women lacked the finances to promote their own work, women's writing was limited to very small audiences. With so few people reading the work of women, and so few women being encouraged to write, there was little opportunity for the work of female writers to become known and respected. In more recent times, these same problems have confronted many black writers. Such economic factors can shape literary judgments by making the work of certain groups "invisible" to critics.

Practice

1. Here is a list of criteria the English Critics frequently applied in their evaluation of literary works. At first glance, the items might seem straightforward. But they assume that everyone will agree about the meaning of certain terms, and the values to be applied.

Challenge each of the following items by posing questions about it in the right-hand column. The first item has been completed to help you to get started.

"Great Works" must:	Challenges:
provide an insight into life;	Whose life? What is "insight"?
deal with serious themes;	
offer a moral message;	
have an emotional impact;	
be skillfully written;	
have a balance of traditional and original features.	

2. Even those who support the concept of "Great Works" find it hard to agree on a list of titles. Here, however, are some examples of texts which currently might be classified as "Great Works" (although Brontë's position is not secure), with a comparison list of "others." How many titles do you recognize on each list? How many have you read? Which have you enjoyed? (Check off your selections.)

"Greats"

☐ Charles Dickens, *Hard Times*
☐ Jane Austen, *Pride and Prejudice*
☐ William Shakespeare, *Hamlet*
☐ Thomas Hardy, *The Mayor of Casterbridge*
☐ Joseph Conrad, *Heart of Darkness*
☐ John Dryden, *Absolom and Achitophel*
☐ Alexander Pope, *Essays on Man*
☐ Henry James, *The Ambassadors*
☐ Emily Brontë, *Wuthering Heights*
☐ James Joyce, *Ulysses*

"Others"

☐ A. A. Milne, *Winnie the Pooh*
☐ Agatha Christie, *Murder on the Orient Express*
☐ Margaret Mitchell, *Gone with the Wind*
☐ Bram Stoker, *Dracula*
☐ Alice Walker, *The Color Purple*

- ☐ Harold Robbins, *Never Love a Stranger*
- ☐ Virginia Andrews, *Flowers in the Attic*
- ☐ Sally Morgan, *My Place*
- ☐ Stephen King, *The Shining*
- ☐ Frank Herbert, *Dune*
- ☐ Elizabeth Jolley, *Cabin Fever*
- ☐ Douglas Adams, *The Hitch-Hiker's Guide to the Galaxy*

3. Here is an alternative list of criteria for "Great Works." Indicate those which might be proposed as explanations for the differences between the two lists of books. Then discuss how neutral the English Critics' criteria seem to be.

☐ writer must be dead?	☐ archaic or difficult language?
☐ writer preferably British?	☐ not widely popular?
☐ writer preferably male?	☐ require specialist knowledge?
☐ writer preferably white?	☐ written for adult readers?

Summary

English Criticism is a general term for the kind of criticism which dominated English universities from the mid 1920s and is still influential today. It emphasized the judgment of literary works on the basis of timeless values, and established a canon of "Great Works."

See also: author
literature
criticism

English Criticism

Feminist Criticism

To get you thinking

■ Can you solve this riddle?

A father and son are involved in a car accident while out driving. The father is killed, but the boy survives and is rushed to the hospital for emergency surgery. The surgeon looks briefly at the boy, and then calls for another doctor, saying, "I cannot operate on this boy, because he is my son."

■ Who is the surgeon?

Theory

Feminist criticism is especially concerned with the way gender assumptions, especially about women, operate in the reading and writing of literary texts. They wish to show how literary texts either sustain or challenge the structure of *patriarchy*—a social system in which power is kept in the hands of men.

Feminist critics argue that gender inequalities are reproduced at three levels:

■ in the production of texts;
■ in the structure and language of texts;
■ and through reading practices.

The production of texts is gendered because the "means of production"—publishing houses, printing presses, bookshops— traditionally have been owned by men. This has made the publishing industry more receptive to stories which support masculine views of life.

The language and structure of texts reproduce gender inequalities by marginalizing femininity. The use of the male pronoun *he* as the general term for *human being* is one way in which this occurs. Another factor is the emphasis on male "heroes" in popular narratives. In many stories, female characters become merely the "obstacles" or "prizes" which the male protagonists encounter during the narrative. Women are reduced to the status of objects, whereas men are the characters who matter.

Reading practices combine with these textual structures to reinforce inequalities. Dominant reading practices encourage readers to "identify" with characters in a story. In mainstream narratives, readers have the choice of identifying with the active, masterful male "hero" or the passive, helpless, pretty "heroine." Male readers are therefore better catered for than female readers: they can *identify* with the hero (imagine *being* him) and *desire* the heroine (imagine *having* her). The choice for women readers is less clear cut. They must choose either to identify with subordinate character positions, or to identify with male characters.

In order to disrupt these processes, feminist critics advocate two courses of action. One is to read "against the grain": to deliberately challenge the text by pointing out its gender inequalities. The second course of action is to promote texts (whether written by men or women) which do not reproduce traditional concepts of gender.

Practice

Many texts make use of stereotyped representations which place women in one of four categories:

1. nurturing mothers/carers;
2. dutiful daughters;
3. sexual/passionate women;
4. mad/bad women.

In Western cultures, the first two are read as "legitimate" positions; the third represents a possible position at certain times, while the last represents a nonconforming position. These categories have been argued to define women in terms of what men want from them.

1. Show which categories stereotypical representations of the following characters might belong to, by writing the appropriate number or numbers.

☐ Barmaids	☐ Nurses and schoolmistresses
☐ Successful businesswomen	☐ Prostitutes
☐ "Adulterous" women	☐ "Childless" women
☐ Unmarried mothers	☐ Secretaries
☐ Nuns	☐ Actors

2. Often female characters move from one category to another in the course of a story. An example of this can be seen in the folktale of "Rapunzel," which is summarized below.

Rapunzel was a beautiful young girl who lived in the care of an old witch. The witch kept Rapunzel shut up in a high tower which had no stairs. To get into the tower, the witch would command Rapunzel to let down her long hair, and the witch would climb up. Seeing this one day, the King's son waited until the witch had gone, called for Rapunzel to let down her hair, and climbed up. Rapunzel saw that the prince was handsome, and promised herself to him. She told the prince to visit her each evening and bring a silk scarf, which she would weave into a rope so that they both could leave the tower. One day the witch learned of the prince's visits. She cut off Rapunzel's hair and cast her into the wilderness. In his grief, the prince fell from the tower and was blinded by thorns. Both the prince and Rapunzel lived in their separate grief, until one day they chanced upon each other in the forest. Rapunzel wept for the prince, and her tears fell on his eyes and restored his sight. They married, and lived happily ever after with their two children.

What are the three categories through which Rapunzel passes?

1.
2.
3.

Which of the four categories does the witch belong in?

3. How well does Rapunzel's pathway match:

▪ the typical romance story?
▪ ideas of girlhood/womanhood in your culture?

4. Do the women in this text represent obstacles and prizes? How?
5. Would this text normally be read as supporting or challenging the patriarchal oppression of women?

Summary

Feminist criticism is concerned with the relationship between literary texts/readings and the place of women in society. It uses its critical methods to demonstrate, explain, and challenge the oppression of women.

See also: gender
reading practices

(Riddle solution: *The surgeon is the boy's mother.*)

Feminist Criticism

Figurative Language

To get you thinking

■ Can you say what two things are being compared in each of the following phrases?

Phrase	Elements		
My love is like a red, red rose.	Lover	&	flower
The moon was a ghostly galleon tossed upon cloudy seas.	_____	&	_____
The minister waddled up to the speaker's platform, ruffled his plumage importantly, and addressed the crowd.	_____	&	_____
Shared beliefs are the foundation of any society.	_____	&	_____
The old man in the corner was well known for spinning yarns.	_____	&	_____

■ Are these "special" uses of language? Would you find any of them in everyday conversation?

Theory

The term "figurative" language has traditionally referred to language which differs from everyday, "nonliterary" usage. Figures were seen as stylistic ornaments with which writers dressed up their language to make it more entertaining, and to clarify the meanings they wanted to convey. According to this view, literary devices such as *metaphor, simile, rhythm,* and so on, embellished "ordinary" language, and so forced readers to work harder at making meaning in a text. Nowadays we recognize that all language is in some sense "figurative": there are very few ways of talking and writing about the world that do not make use of comparisons, symbols, and so on.

The following are some important figures.

Simile

The comparison of two elements, where each maintains its own identity. For example: "My love is like a red, red rose." Here a person is compared to a flower in a way that suggests they have certain features in common, such as beauty, fragility, and so on.

Metaphor

The merging of two elements or ideas, where one is used to modify the meaning of the other. For example: "The moon was a ghostly galleon tossed upon cloudy seas." Here the image of the moon in a cloudy night sky is merged with that of a sailing ship on stormy seas, so that some characteristics of the latter are transferred to the former.

Metonym

The use of a part to represent a whole, or the use of one item to stand for another with which it has become associated. For example, in the news headline "Palace Shocked by Secret Photos," the palace stands for the royal family and their aides.

Personification

The description of a nonhuman force or object in terms of a person or living thing. For example, "The gnarled branches clawed at the clouds." Here, the tree branches are given the characteristics of grasping hands.

Symbol

The substitution of one element for another as a matter of convention rather than similarity. For example, in the biblical story of Adam and Eve, the serpent is used as a symbol of temptation. In the ceremonies of the modern Olympics, white doves symbolize peace and freedom. Language itself is also symbolic, since words and meanings are associated purely by convention.

Because so much of our language is "figurative" rather than literal, there is always room for disagreement about the meanings of words, phrases, and texts. Different groups of readers may well "decode" such language in different ways, according to their beliefs, values, and social practices. In exploring the language of "literary" and "nonliterary" texts, we need to consider the range of readings made possible by figures of speech, and how this range of possibilities is limited or closed off by other features in the text and by specific ways of reading.

Practice

The following extract is from Colin Thiele's story "The Shell." In these passages, some of the figurative language has been set in **bolder** type.

> The green sea swept into the shallows and **seethed** there **like slaking quicklime**. It surged over the rocks, tossing up spangles of water **like a juggler** and catching them deftly again behind. It raced knee deep through the clefts and crevices, twisted and tortured in a thousand ways, till it swept **nuzzling and sucking** into the holes at the base of the cliff.
>
> The shell lay in a saucer of rock. It was a green cowrie, clean and new, **its pink undersides as delicate as human flesh**. All around it the rocks dropped away sheer or **leaned out** in an overhang streaked with dripping strands of **slime like wet hair**. The waves spumed over it, hissing and curling, but the shell **tumbled the water off its back** or just rocked gently **like a bead in the palm of the hand**.

[In the course of the story two fishermen are swept from the rocks by a wave "like a hand." The story concludes with two policemen searching the beach for the bodies.]

> The first man searched down along the shore and stopped near a rock exposed by the ebb. "Look at this shell," he called. "It's a beauty. A green cowrie."
>
> "**Blood money! The sea's buying you off!**" He watched distastefully as the first man reached down and closed his fingers beneath the smooth pink underside of the shell, **as delicate as human flesh**. And the sea came **gurgling** gently round his shoes, **like a cat** rubbing its back against his legs.

[Note: quicklime = a fizzy, acid solution]

1. Quote words or phrases from the extract as follows:

Figures	Quotations
A phrase which *personifies* the sea	
A *simile* which makes the sea seem playful	
A *metaphor* which compares the sea to a baby	
A *simile* which makes the sea seem calculating	
A *symbol* of trading	

2. What characteristics are given to the sea by these comparisons? Make your selections by matching items from the two lists below.

Comparison	Characteristics
The juggler	capricious (changeable, selfish)
The baby	ruthless
The trader	innocent, not responsible
Quicklime	skillful, playful
The cat	damaging

Can these items be matched up in more than one combination? Is there room for disagreement about what figurative expressions might mean?

3. Which of the following reasons might explain why the sea has been characterized as a living thing?

- because it makes the story more entertaining?
- because Western cultures see life in terms of a competition between humans and nature?
- because it provides a mythical explanation for events that otherwise seem meaningless?
- the characterization is purely accidental?

Summary

Figurative language is that which provides the reader with comparisons, substitutions, and patterns that shape meaning. Literary texts sometimes make concentrated use of figurative language. However, most language is figurative in some sense, because words do not have single, objective meanings.

See also: imagery

Figurative Language

Foregrounding and Privileging

To get you thinking

■ In the space below, write the meaning these words have in "everyday" use. (Use a dictionary if you are unsure.)

foreground:

privilege:

■ Underneath these definitions, indicate how these terms might be applied to the study of literary texts. What could they refer to?

Theory

In every text we read, some features seem more obvious or prominent than others. This kind of *emphasis* is often explained with the terms *foregrounding* and *privileging*. We can say that foregrounding refers to the emphasis placed on certain features of the text (words, phrases, and so on), whereas privileging refers to the degree of importance attached to particular meanings.

Particular elements of a text are not foregrounded or privileged by the text itself. They are the combined effect of ways of organizing the text (textual organization) and ways of reading (reading practices).

Certain features in a text may be emphasized through a variety of techniques, including the selection of detail, repetition, exaggeration, and contrast. When some aspects of a text are emphasized in this way, we say that the concepts they refer to have been foregrounded.

For example:

In this extract from Charles Dickens's novel, *Hard Times*, repetition and selection of detail have been used to foreground the "mechanical" style of the teacher, Mr. Thomas Gradgrind. (The scene is set in a nineteenth-century schoolroom.)

"Now, what I want is, Facts. Teach these boys and girls nothing but Facts. Facts alone are wanted in life. Plant nothing else, and root out everything else. You can only form the minds of reasoning animals upon Facts: nothing else will ever be of service to them . . ."

The scene was a plain bare monotonous vault of a schoolroom, and the speaker's forefinger emphasised his observations by underscoring every sentence with a line on the schoolmaster's sleeve . . .

"Girl number twenty," said Mr. Gradgrind, squarely pointing with his square forefinger, "I don't know that girl. Who is that girl?"
   "Sissy Jupe sir," explained number twenty, blushing, standing up, and curtseying.
   "Sissy is not a name," said Mr. Gradgrind. "Don't call yourself Sissy. Call yourself Cecilia."

We could say that this extract foregrounds the rigid discipline of Thomas Gradgrind's approach to teaching through repetition ("Facts") and through details such as the numbering of the students.

Dickens's novel is often read as an attack on "cold and unfeeling" forms of education. Read in this way, the text seems to place a higher value on emotions and relationships than on "cold facts." That is, in foregrounding the "mechanical," it *privileges* the personal/humane. However, different readings of the text might place the emphasis elsewhere. To a culture which values factual knowledge over feelings, this text might seem to offer a positive image of rigorous instruction. In such a reading, the same textual details might be *foregrounded*, but an opposing set of values would be *privileged*.

By exploring a text in terms of forgrounding and privileging, we can begin to see how certain attitudes and values are promoted by particular readings.

Practice

This next extract is from Joseph Conrad's novel *Heart of Darkness*, a text which is now seen as offensively racist in many respects. It is narrated by Charlie Marlowe, the captain of a steamer traveling down the Congo during the European invasion of Africa.

> Now and then a boat from the shore gave one a momentary contact with reality. It was paddled by black fellows. You could see from afar the white of their eyeballs glistening. They shouted, sang; their bodies steamed with perspiration; they had faces like grotesque masks—these chaps; but they had bone, muscle, a wild vitality, an intense energy that was as natural and true as the surf along their coast. They wanted no excuse for being there. They were a great comfort to look at.

1. This description of the people in the boat can be read as *foregrounding* physical appearance. It describes the people as mere bodies, as something "to be looked at." Underline the words and phrases from the passage which emphasise the physical appearance of the people. For example, "the white of their eyeballs."
2. European culture has traditionally privileged the mind over body. Mind and "spirit" have been regarded as having a higher value than the body. In this passage, the foregrounding of the Africans' bodies has a number of effects:

   ▪ it obscures the mental and spiritual qualities of the Africans;
   ▪ by associating the Africans with nature (the surf) it sets them up as a "reverse image" of the European narrator (who therefore represents "culture");
   ▪ it constructs the narrator as "mind" rather than body.

Through this process the Africans are "made visible," while the European captain remains hidden and escapes description and judgment. In this way the European perspective is privileged, and readers are invited to take up this privileged position. We can demonstrate this by asking some questions of the passage. Indicate your answers to the questions below: African or European?

Who looks or sees in the passage?   Who takes comfort?
Who is looked at or seen?   Who is comfort taken from?
Who "knows" in the passage?   Who is presented as body?
Who is "known"?   Who is presented as mind?

Which of these positions has the most power?

3. Which of the following might be effective ways of counteracting these effects of privileging? Rank the possibilities from 1 (most effective) to 5 (least effective).

☐ Alternating the narration between two points of view—African and European.
☐ Refusing to read the book.
☐ Remembering that the work is fictional, and arguing that it has no effect on the "real world."
☐ Publishing and promoting African accounts of the European invasion.
☐ Reading "against the grain"—reading the book as racist propaganda by foregrounding the European's role and privileging the Africans' perspective.

What difficulties might there be in these courses of action?

Summary

Foregrounding refers to an emphasis placed on certain features of the text (words, phrases, and so on), whereas privileging refers to the promotion of particular values and meanings. Foregrounding and privileging are the combined effects of textual organization and reading practices.

See also: readings
reading practices

Foregrounding and Privileging

Gaps and Silences

To get you thinking

▪ Can you make sense of these passages by filling in the gaps?

As sound waves travel _____ the air they enter _____ ears and bump against _____ ear drum. The ear _____ is made of extremely _____, sensitive skin and the _____ waves make it vibrate. _____ nerves in the skin _____ the vibrations and pass _____ message to the brain.

(Sensations, WA Education Dept.)

Mr Jones, of the _____ Farm, had locked the hen-houses _____ the night, but was _____ drunk to remember to _____ the pop-holes. With the ring _____ light from his lantern _____ from side to side, _____ lurched across the yard, _____ off his boots at _____ back door, drew himself a glass of _____ from the barrel in the _____, and made his _____ up to bed, where Mrs _____ was already snoring.

(Animal Farm, George Orwell)

▪ What factors enable you to "make sense" of the text? Is it the structure of the text itself, your own knowledge and experiences, or a combination of the two?
▪ What similarities are there between this activity and the "normal" process of reading?

Theory

No text can offer its readers a complete and balanced "window on the world." Texts are made up of elements selected from a cultural system, such as language, and arranged according to certain conventions. In this way, texts are like the toys that children make out of blocks and constructor sets. The objects they make are only rough approximations of houses, cars, and airplanes. What makes these things meaningful is the information supplied by the child: memories, imagination, playfulness.

Like these toy houses, texts offer only a particular impression or version of reality, shaped by the basic elements from which they are made. For a text to mean anything at all, readers must apply a set of procedures to "decode" the signs and fill in background information. Readers make meaning with texts by supplying readings that are already available in the culture. A line such as: "he behaved like a prince," for example, invites readers to make use of a range of memories and beliefs about princes, romantic love, men and women, and so on.

The "spaces" of a text can be described in many ways. Modern approaches often speak of them as "gaps and silences." *Gaps* are places where the text does not bother to stitch things together but instead relies on "common sense" assumptions from the reader. For example, here is an extract from a news report.

> Miss Smith is the second girl to be reported missing this week. She was last seen hitchhiking along a city street late on Monday afternoon.
> Police have issued a warning to young girls not to go out alone at night.

These sentences do not say outright that there was a connection between Miss Smith's hitchhiking and her disappearance; it is assumed that readers will make the connection. But the link is not obvious. It relies on very specific cultural knowledge about "the way the world works." In order to construct the dominant reading of this passage, readers must assume:

- that the girl was kidnapped while walking;
- that she was kidnapped by a male;
- that this would be less likely to happen if she was accompanied;
- that she was taking a risk by hitchhiking; and so on.

If we resist the invitation to fill this gap with the conventional assumptions, the text's incompleteness becomes very obvious. It then becomes clear that the message requires readers to reproduce "unconsciously" a very strange set of assumptions about what "natural" behavior is!

Silences result from the fact that textual gaps enable readers to avoid questioning certain cultural values. In the above example, the text remains silent about the behavior and motivations of *men*, even though it could have been written by a woman or a man. This has the double effect of making safety on the streets a woman's problem, and of vaguely implicating all men in the disappearance. The text could have said: Police have issued a warning for *men* not to go out at night. This would certainly make the streets safer.

In fact, by substituting this statement for the original, we can make ourselves aware of many silences in this text. By mapping these silences we can reveal that the text operates in the interest of some groups in the community, and against the interest of others.

Practice

This extract comes from "The Doll's House" by Katherine Mansfield. (The letters and **bolder** type refer to the activities that follow.)

> [T]he school the Burnell children went to was (A) **not at all the kind of place their parents would have chosen** if there had been any choice. But there was none. It was the only school for miles. And the consequence was that (B) **all the children in the neighborhood, the Judge's little girls, the doctor's daughters, the storekeeper's children, the milkman's, were forced to mix together**. But the line had to be drawn somewhere. It was drawn at the Kelveys. Many of the children, including the Burnells, (C) **were not even allowed to speak to them**. Even the teachers had a special voice for them, and a special smile for the other children when Lil Kelvey came up to her desk with a bunch of (D) **dreadfully common looking flowers**.

Like all texts, this one requires readers to supply a great deal of knowledge in order to "make sense" of the writing. The **bolder type** sections of text highlight gaps which readers fill on the basis of "common sense." What information must readers supply in order to produce the dominant reading of this passage? (Some possible readings of the **bolder type** sections are provided below. Use them to fill in the table.)

"Gap"	Information
(A)	_____
(B)	_____
(C)	_____
(D)	_____

Possible readings:

i.   children can be harmed by association with those whose values and behavior are different to their own;

ii. gifts can be judged in terms of the social standing of the person who gives them;

iii. society is divided into "class" groups on the basis of wealth and status, which equate with the (male?) parent's profession;

iv. some schools have a higher social standing than others, and these are sought after by parents of high social standing.

We can sum up the "missing information" in this way: "Members of a culture try to maintain or improve their social standing, and avoid associating with those of significantly lower class." The text itself does *not* include this information, however. This suggests that such knowledge functions as "common sense" among members of our culture. By assuming that all readers can supply this information, the text can remain *silent* about the question of social class. It presents class snobbery as a problem of personal beliefs and attitudes, and so fails to challenge those aspects of social organization which are the basis of class divisions.

Summary

Gaps are places in the text where readers are invited to make connections by drawing on their "common sense" understanding of the world. *Silences* result from the fact that textual gaps enable readers to avoid questioning certain cultural values.

See also: reading practices
ideology

Gaps and Silences

Gender

To get you thinking

■ Here are some assertions about differences between men and women. For each statement, check whether you think the difference is due to biology or culture.

	Biology	Culture
Women can give birth; men cannot.	☐	☐
Men are more aggressive than women.	☐	☐
Men are stronger than women.	☐	☐
Women are better at childrearing than men.	☐	☐
Women are less competitive than men.	☐	☐
Men find it harder to be monogamous than women.	☐	☐

■ Do you think all of these statements are true? Which, if any, would you challenge?

Theory

We all know that there are some basic biological differences between the sexes. But there are also a great many differences created by culture which have nothing to do with biology. These cultural factors are called *gender* differences.

Primary sex differences between males and females remain the same in all cultures. Gender differences vary greatly from one culture to another. In Western societies, males are expected to be active, competitive, domineering, and authoritative. Women are expected to be passive, cooperative, submissive, and caring. But these masculine and feminine characteristics are completely reversed in some societies. This shows that the differences are not "natural," but cultural.

In the activity above, you were making distinctions between sex and gender. In many areas of society, these distinctions are hidden, with the result that gender differences are often thought to be "natural"—like a person's anatomy. The problem with this is that gender is used as a means of social organization. It is a technique for producing inequalities between men and women.

Cultures create gender through social practices such as education, employment, and childrearing. These activities slot men and women into different positions of power. Traditionally, women have been raised to take on domestic roles such as wife and mother, while men have been prepared for more powerful positions as wage earners and decision makers. They have even been given personality characteristics which match these positions.

These "dividing practices" are supported by myths about the "natural" differences between men and women. In our culture, novels, plays, films, and other kinds of text have been important in maintaining these myths. They encourage us to believe that there are naturally occurring moral, intellectual, and emotional differences between males and females. By reading such stories as "reflections of life," people come to accept their images of men and women as natural. This is why it is important to challenge both the texts we read and the way we have been trained to read them.

Practice

Here are two very common storylines which reinforce dominant beliefs about men and women.

An ambitious young woman decides to pursue a career rather than marry and have a family. She works hard, and achieves her goal, but despite her success she is unhappy. She realizes that she no longer has any friends. Then, she meets a stranger in unusual circumstances. After initially disliking each other, she and the man fall in love. Happy at last, the woman gives up her career and settles down to raise a family.

A sensitive young man suffers at the hands of his male colleagues, who tease him because of his gentleness. The women where he works treat him as a joke. One day, he meets up with a very shy, plain-looking woman. They fall in love, and for the first time the young man begins to feel wanted. Then, in unusual circumstances, the woman is placed in danger. The young man risks his life to save her, and in the process proves himself braver than his colleagues. His life is changed. People treat him with new respect, he gains a promotion, and marries his sweetheart, who takes off her glasses, lets down her hair, and is revealed to be very beautiful.

1. Stories of this kind are structured around pairs of ideas about what men and women should be like. Suggest some of the oppositions which are supported by these storylines by filling in this table.

Masculine	Feminine
career-oriented	family-oriented

2. Here are some cultural practices which slot people into masculine and feminine roles. Number the items from 1 to 12, indicating which ones you think are most obvious, and which are the least obvious, in shaping gender.

Sport & recreation   Common sayings   School subjects
Children's toys   Codes of dress   Religious practices
Family structures   "Literary" texts   Children's games
Traditions(e.g.,marriage)   Fairytales   Occupations

3. Which factors do you think might be most powerful, and hardest to change—those which are obvious, or those which are largely unnoticed? Why?

Summary

Gender refers to the social categories of masculinity and femininity. These categories are related to sex differences in complex ways, but they are produced by culture, not biology.

See also: feminist criticism
representation

Gender

Genre

To get you thinking

◼ Sort these items into groups by applying the rules below.

apple	bananas	cauliflower	tomatoes
potatoes	beans	peanuts	cabbage
lettuce	avocado	carrots	zucchini

◼ Sort by *features*. Choose two categories (e.g., "fruits"/"vegetables," or "above ground"/"below ground").
◼ Sort by *use*. Choose two categories (e.g., "eat raw"/"cook" or "main meal"/"snack").

Theory

Genre comes from the French language and means a kind or type. In literature study it often refers to different categories of writing. Traditionally, the major genres were poetry, prose, and drama. These broad types of writing were distinguished by their features, and they were often broken down into subgenres. Poetry, for example, might be subdivided into "lyric" and "epic." We can also speak of different genres within a particular medium. Common film genres, for example, are: Western, romance, horror, thriller, action movie, and so on.

Categorizing texts in this way is more complicated than it seems. This is because texts are not simply classified on the basis of their features, but on the basis of rules for reading that are shared by the members of a community. This is similar to the way fruit and vegetables are classified. Some communities regard the tomato as a fruit, and hardly ever cook it; others see the tomato as a vegetable, and rarely eat it raw. In the past, some people believed it to be a deadly poison, and did not eat it at all. In a similar way, the reading practices which prevail in a community will provide a range of "genre categories" through which texts will be read.

For example, we can see this in David Lynch's TV series *Twin Peaks*. Released in the late 1980s, *Twin Peaks* was read by some people as a comedy, by others as a soap opera, by others as a satire. The series contained features which supported a range of generic readings, and people made sense of it by applying rules that were most familiar to them. This suggests that texts are always read "through" genre—that genres are like colored spectacles that we can change but never remove. They are rules which always *limit* the way writers and readers construct meaning in texts, but which are essential in *enabling* us to read at all.

The reason for raising issues of genre when studying a text is that genre categories function to promote certain values by shaping our reading practices. This can have a powerful effect on the meanings which readers produce. It is important to note that genres are tied to the activities of certain institutions, such as publishing houses, schools, and the media. These institutions organize their production and use of texts through genres. Publishers market their books in categories (fantasy, romance, thriller). Schools and universities often plan courses of study around genres (tragic drama, lyric poetry, the short story). The media produce and promote texts through genre (soap operas on TV, human interest stories in news broadcasts). In each case, genre enables and constrains the reading of the text.

Practice

Here is a brief summary of the folktale "Little Red Riding Hood."

- Mother sends RRH to grandma's house.
- She warns RRH not to leave the path and not to talk to strangers.
- RRH meets the wolf, who asks where she is going.
- The wolf gets to grandma's house first, and eats the old woman.
- When RRH arrives, she notices grandma's unusual appearance.
- The wolf reveals that he plans to eat RRH.
- A passing woodcutter rescues RRH and slays the wolf.

1. Which features of the "Red Riding Hood" story would be emphasized if the following genre categories were applied to it? Match the "genre" with a possible emphasis below.

Genre	Emphasis
Horror	the woodcutter's rescue
Mystery	the killing of grandma, the wolf
Fantasy	the talking, scheming wolf
Moral fable	the disguised wolf
Romance	the danger of leaving the path

2. How does each genre "contain" or construct femininity, through the image of the young girl in the story? Suggest genre categories which might promote these readings. Use the list above to get you started in filling in the following chart.

Reading	Genres
RRH is a helpless female who needs to be rescued by a capable man.	
RRH is an "innocent" girl who must keep herself safe from predatory creatures.	
RRH is a perceptive girl who quickly sees through the wolf's disguise, and so shows she can take care of herself.	

Summary

Genres are categories set up by the interaction of textual features and reading practices, which shape and limit the meanings readers can make with a text.

See also: conventions

text

"reading" entries

Genre

Identification

To get you thinking

■ Using a table layout, make a list of some people you think are a lot like you, or who you want to be like. List the reasons for your choice in the right-hand column.

Person   Reasons

Movie star:
Friend, relative:
Fictional character:

Theory

Identification is a psychological term. It describes a process in which people develop a sense of who they are by forming relationships with those whom they admire or wish to be like. Small children, for example, often seem to model their behavior on that of parents and friends. Adults, too, might emulate the views of people they admire—whether these are personal acquaintances, or even famous public figures. When people form such attachments, we can say that they *identify* with the other person.

In reading stories and watching films, a similar process seems to occur, and so it is common to speak of readers *identifying* (or forming an *identification*) with the main character in a novel. This happens when features in the text combine with reading practices in order to "equate" the reader with the character. This kind of identification plays a powerful role in reproducing certain values and beliefs.

For example, many "thriller" movies contain scenes in which a young woman alone is being stalked by an unseen pursuer. In these scenes the camera generally places the viewer in the position of the hidden assailant: we see the frightened woman "through the assailant's eyes." In this way, the viewer is positioned alongside, or "equated to" the assailant. This matching up of viewer and character directs attention away from the assailant and onto the potential victim. In this way, readers are encouraged to produce a reading in which the woman's distress—rather than the assailant's motive—becomes the focus of the plot.

Many people want to challenge this kind of reading, and this is why some modern approaches to literary study (such as feminism) emphasize the importance of reading "against the grain" and refusing to identify with the reading position that is offered.

Practice

Here are two extracts from John Fowles's novel *The Collector*. The story concerns a young man who kidnaps and imprisons a woman he is infatuated with. The first extract is narrated by the man, Frederick Clegg.

> That was the day I first gave myself the dream that came true. It began where she was being attacked by a man and I ran up and rescued her. Then somehow I was the man who attacked her, only I didn't hurt her; I captured her and drove her off in the van to a remote house and there I kept her captive in a nice way. Gradually she came to know me and like me and the dream grew into the one about our living in a nice modern house, married, with kids and everything.

1. In what ways do textual features and reading practices (ways of reading) encourage identification with Frederick Clegg in this passage? Consider, for example, how the reading might be changed if the object of Clegg's "dream" were a child.

This second extract is narrated by the woman, Miranda Grey, who is kidnapped and imprisoned by Frederick Clegg and who dies of pneumonia as a result:

> Deep down I get more and more frightened. I wish I knew judo. Could make him cry for mercy. I feel the deepest contempt and loathing for him, I can't stand this room, everybody will be wild with worry. How can he love me? How can you love someone you don't know? He desperately wants to please me, but that's what madmen must be like. . . . I'm so frightened. I can't understand why my chest hurts. As if I've had bronchitis for days. But he'd have to get a doctor. He might kill me, but he couldn't just let me die. Oh, God, this is horrible.

2. Here is a list of statements readers might support. Readers who identify with Frederick Clegg will support some; readers who identify with Miranda Grey will support others. Indicate with FC or MG the statements which might be supported in each case.

Deeds must be judged in terms of a person's intentions.   _____

Intentions must be weighed against consequences.   _____

Clegg's actions can be seen as chivalrous and romantic.   _____

Clegg's actions are immoral and criminal.   _____

Women secretly want to be "swept away" by men.   _____

Domination is unacceptable in any relationship.   _____

3. To what extent does the use of two points of view help to overcome the problem of identification?
4. Consider these questions in relation to the double point of view:

■ Will readers construct a balanced and neutral reading of the story, or will one character's point of view tend to dominate?
■ If so, which one, and why?
■ Will this be true for all readers?

Summary

Identification occurs when textual features and reading practices combine to construct an equivalence between the reader and characters in the text. When this happens, the values and beliefs of the text and the reader reinforce each other.

See also: character

Identification

Ideology

To get you thinking

■ Whose views seem to be expressed by these common beliefs? Check your choice in each box.

Belief	Viewpoint
Material possessions are important for a happy life.	☐ Manufacturers ☐ Consumers
Men are the stronger sex; women should let them take charge of things.	☐ Men ☐ Women
There are right and wrong ways of reading a literary text.	☐ Casual readers ☐ Critics

■ How can you explain the fact that such beliefs are often thought to be true even by people they might work *against*?

Theory

People often use the term *ideology* to refer to *someone else's* political beliefs: for example, "socialist ideology." This implies that the other person's beliefs are false or biased, and that one's own beliefs are true and neutral. But are there any "neutral" beliefs and values?

Groups of people who share similar interests develop specific ways of looking at the world. Manufacturers might see the world in terms of profit and loss; workers might see it in terms of fair payment and exploitation; priests might see it in terms of good and evil.

Some theories of culture argue that powerful groups can succeed in passing on their view of the world to others, so that one way of thinking tends to dominate. In this way, groups of people come to think and act in particular ways, even though those ways may not serve their best interests. They might even come to think of this as a "natural" state of affairs.

"Ideology" can be said to refer to ways of thinking and acting which work to the advantage of particular groups of people, but which are thought to be neutral or "natural" and true.

Ideologies are spread from one group to another through cultural practices such as education, employment, marketing, and childraising, and through texts such as novels and films. This can occur because the control of these practices is generally in the hands of particular groups of people. Their values are reproduced and passed on to people as "knowledge." In the case of literature, the values of white, Anglo-Saxon, middle-class males have tended to dominate, because these are the people who exercised control over schooling, publishing, and so on. Thus, much of what was claimed to be objective literary "knowledge" was ideological. Today there is a greater diversity among theories of literature, but competing theories all serve specific interests. There are *no* neutral approaches to literature.

Ideologies can be resisted. When groups of people begin systematically to study their place in society, they may begin to question the values they have been taught to live by. Movements such as Marxism and feminism are examples of this process. The theories and practices of these groups are aimed at overturning the *dominant* ideology in favor of new forms of social organization and new values or ideologies.

Practice

This is an extract from the Declaration of Independence, drafted by Thomas Jefferson in the 1770s. It is intended to reflect a set of neutral beliefs and values.

> We hold these truths to be self-evident, that all men are created equal, that they are endowed by their Creator with certain unalienable rights, that among these are life, liberty and the pursuit of happiness.

1. Underline parts of the text which can be read as implying the following ideologies:

   ■ gender ideology   ■ religious ideology   ■ political ideology

2. In whose interests do these ideologies generally operate? (Circle your choices.)

Gender ideology: men? women?
Religious ideology: atheists? Christians? pantheists?
Political ideology: conservatives who believe in absolute truths? radicals who believe "truth" is always a question of politics?

3. Which of the following behaviors might be supported by the dominant reading of the extract above from the Declaration of Independence?

- going to church?
- teaching the theory of evolution?
- overthrowing the leaders of a nondemocratic country?
- fighting a war?

4. Does this document work to bring about "equality," or does it divide people into groups?

Summary

Ideologies are systems of thought and action which work to the advantage of particular groups of people and which might be shared even by people who are disadvantaged by them.

See also: class
           feminist criticism
           Marxist criticism

Ideology

Imagery

To get you thinking

■ Here are some extracts from "famous" poems. Read each one through a number of times, then number them from 1 to 4, according to which extracts give you the most vivid "mental picture" of the thing described.

Poem extract	Ranking
My heart is like an apple-tree Whose boughs are bent with thickset fruit . . . [Christina G. Rossetti]	
Let us go then, you and I, When the evening is spread out against the sky Like a patient etherized upon a table . . . [T. S. Eliot]	
Day after day, day after day, We stuck, nor breath nor motion; As idle as a painted ship upon a painted ocean . . . [Samuel Taylor Coleridge]	
The wind was a torrent of darkness among the gusty trees, The moon was a ghostly galleon tossed upon cloudy seas . . . [Alfred Noyes]	

■ Are the "mental pictures" generated by the words themselves, or do they rely upon your own experiences and memories?

■ Can you be sure that the images you "see" are the same as those of another reader?

Theory

The term *imagery* has many meanings in literary study. One popular use refers to "mental pictures" which some readers claim are conjured up when they read certain poems—especially those which describe or represent physical objects. These descriptions might be "direct," or they might make use of various literary "devices," such as simile or metaphor.

For example, a tree in winter might be described a number of ways: "bare of leaves, outlined against the sky"; or "a fork of black lightning, frozen into permanence against the white clouds." The first description uses no obvious comparisons; the second makes use of metaphor.

Imagery is also used in other ways. It can refer to the *pattern* of comparisons or descriptions in a text. For example, many of Shakespeare's plays repeat images of disease, which can be read as supporting the tragic storyline. The term can also be applied to descriptions which do not describe objects, but which refer to senses of touch, hearing, taste, or smell.

All of these uses have the following in common: they assume that techniques of description used in a text are important to the meaning of the work; and they assume that competent readers should agree about the *effect* of such descriptions. Some modern approaches to literature accept these assumptions, but others point out that "imagery" is partly a question of how texts are *read*. Newspaper articles, which we often think of being written in "ordinary" language, also contain images; but when reading newspapers we tend to read for "facts" rather than "technique."

Emphasis on imagery is very strong in a kind of criticism called *New Criticism*. This approach to literature argues that the emotional effects created by poetry and other texts should not rely on the feelings of the author or the reader but should be "objectified" in "concrete" images. This assumes that a certain image should evoke the same emotional response in all competent readers—a position which disregards the differences of education, class, race, sex, and social position among readers.

When examining the imagery of a text we should consider how the descriptions relate to the beliefs and values of the culture which produced the text, and the culture in which it circulates and is read. But we shouldn't fall into the trap of thinking that patterns of imagery somehow reveal the "true" meaning of a literary work. Rather, our own reading practices will often determine the kind of imagery we "find" in the text.

Practice

This is a sonnet by William Shakespeare. It can be read as a poem about aging and death.

> That time of year thou may'st in me behold
> When yellow leaves, or none, or few, do hang
> Upon those boughs which shake against the cold,
> Bare ruined choirs where late the sweet birds sang.
> In me thou see'st the twilight of such day
> As after sunset fadeth in the west;
> Which by and by black night doth take away,
> Death's second self, that seals up all in rest.
> In me thou see'st the glowing of such fire,
> That on the ashes of his youth doth lie,
> As the deathbed whereon it must expire,
> Consumed with that which it was nourished by.
> This thou perceiv'st, which makes thy love more strong,
> To love that well which thou must leave ere long.

[choirs: the seating in a church where the choir sings; it implies an image of church buildings in ruin, like the bare branches of trees.]

1. Underline words or phrases in the poem that can be read as:

   ▣ images of a particular season (double underline);
   ▣ images of a specific time of day (single);
   ▣ images suggesting an extinguished flame (dotted underline).

2. The following are possible ways of reading the above images. Put a check or a cross by the statements with which you agree or disagree.

   ☐ The images are all metaphors for old age and death.
   ☐ The images complement one another, and are part of a pattern.
   ☐ Some images imply cycles of time, others imply a definite beginning and end.
   ☐ The images contradict one another, sometimes implying that death is final, sometimes implying that it is not.
   ☐ The images progress from large scales of time to small scales, and from circular time to linear time.

Which readings have you supported? Why?

3. In Shakespeare's day, Christian ideas of death were dominant. The Christian view sees death merely as the end of earthly life; it is believed that the soul lives on. The idea of death as final is opposed to Christian teachings. Indicate whether the following references can be read as supporting the dominant (D) or oppositional (O) view.

- ◼ images of season;
- ◼ images of a dying fire;
- ◼ images of twilight;
- ◼ the image of ruined choirs;
- ◼ the comparison of death with night and sleep.

This suggests that Shakespeare's sonnet reflects a particular historical debate about the nature of death.

4. On the basis of your reading of the poem, indicate which of the following statements you would support.

- ◼ The poem supports the Christian view of the world.
- ◼ The poem uses some images which support the Christian view and some which challenge it. It is therefore politically neutral.
- ◼ By including "competing" images the poem raises questions, and is therefore politically radical.
- ◼ The organization of images poses a clear challenge to Christian thinking about death.

Summary

Imagery refers to descriptions of objects and sensations which can be read as representing a particular emotion or idea in the text. With regard to the meaning of a text, the importance of imagery varies according to the reading practices which are being applied.

See also: New Criticism
            representation

Imagery

Intertextuality

To get you thinking

■ Here is a short text which you have not seen before. Can you read it?

It was nine thirty on a wet August morning. The rain rattled like machine-gun fire on the tin roof of the warehouse next door, accompanied by the monotonous *plunk!* of water drops falling into a tin bucket from a leak in the office ceiling. I hadn't had a new case in three weeks. Work was the only thing that had dried up that winter; seemed like even the mobsters had gone into hibernation. I was about ready to do the same when the phone rang. I barely heard it over the rain.

■ Even though you have never seen this particular piece of writing before, you probably had no difficulty making sense of it. This is because the passage contains much that is already familiar, and only a little that is new. Label the following list of features according to whether they were familiar (F) or new (N).

Features   F   N

The meanings of individual words in the passage
The conventions of the "detective" genre
The concepts of character and plot
The rules of narrative (storytelling)
Details about the narrator's present situation

■ Try to imagine a completely original text—one that contained nothing that was familiar to you. Would you be able to read it?

Theory

Although literature study often seems to focus on what is unique, there can be no such thing as a completely original text. All kinds of texts—whether poems, novels, films, or even jokes—gain meaning through their similarities to other texts. If this were not true, readers would be astonished and puzzled by every new text that confronted them: they would have to learn how to read each text using a completely different set of rules.

The term *intertextuality* describes the way texts of all kinds are bound together by the broader reading and writing practices of a culture. The idea becomes clear if we remember that "text" comes from the Latin word "textus"—a woven fabric. We can say that all the individual texts produced in a culture are like designs woven into the larger fabric of language and writing.

Intertextual relationships between works occur at a number of levels. At the most general level are features such as *language*. A great many texts can be constructed from the pool of words and meanings shared by members of a culture. There are also *generic* and *formal* relationships between texts. These are the common conventions and techniques by which we recognize a text as belonging to the category of "detective fiction" or "epic poetry" or "horror film." Finally, there are specific *allusions*—direct quotes or indirect references to other texts, which often invite comparisons.

For example, Jean Rhys's novel *Wide Sargasso Sea* exhibits all of these links. Like most of the texts in Western culture, from motion pictures to limericks, it makes use of the English language, and of narrative techniques. As a novel, it also makes use of conventions such as chapter divisions, characterization, dialogue, and description. And most specifically of all, its characters and plot are related to Charlotte Brontë's nineteenth-century novel, *Jane Eyre*. Rhys's novel tells the story of a character in Brontë's book—Bertha Rochester.

Intertextual links can have the effect of *naturalizing* certain ways of thinking and acting—making them seem normal and innocent. Without being told, you have probably assumed that the character speaking in the brief text at the top of this entry was a man. This information is not "in" the text, but readers "supply" it because detective fiction is related to a set of cultural assumptions about gender, mystery, and mastery. Only if the narrator turned out to be a woman (and she is) would you be surprised. This suggests that many of the "common sense" beliefs and values of our culture are intertextually woven into the fabric of literary works.

Practice

Intertextual references in a work sometimes surprise readers and invite them to question common assumptions. Angela Carter's story "The Company of Wolves" is a retelling of "Little Red Riding Hood." Readers are encouraged to recognize the similarities, and this makes the differences more startling. Here are some extracts from the climax of Angela Carter's story.

> . . . What big teeth you have! She saw how his jaw began to slaver and the room was full of the forest's Liebestod but the wise child never flinched, even when he answered: All the better to eat you with. The girl burst out laughing; she knew she was nobody's meat. She laughed at him full in the face, she ripped off his shirt for him and flung it into the fire . . .
>
> The blizzard died down, leaving the mountains as randomly covered in snow as if a blind woman had thrown a sheet over them . . . See! sweet and sound she sleeps in granny's bed between the paws of the tender wolf.

1. Compare the traditional fairy tale and Carter's retelling of it in the following ways.

   ▪ Describe the difference in language in the stories.
   ▪ Comment on the girl's reaction to the wolf.
   ▪ Describe what becomes of the wolf in each story.
   ▪ Describe what becomes of Granny.
   ▪ Decide who is the "hero" of each story.
   ▪ Suggest the readership that each story is probably aimed at.

2. The intertextual relation that is set up between Angela Carter's story and "Little Red Riding Hood" can have the effect of raising certain issues. Which of the following issues might a reading of "The Company of Wolves" raise?

- social assumptions about women?
- social assumptions about men?
- the role of fairy tales in promoting values and beliefs?
- the different audiences which are addressed by certain genres of writing?
- social attitudes about the treatment of animals?
- social attitudes about children?

3. Which of the following statements would Angela Carter's story seem to support?

- Women are more resourceful than we are led to believe.
- Traditional fairy tales serve the interests of men.
- The folktale genre is suitable only for children.

Summary

Intertextuality refers to the network or web of relationships which underlies all the texts produced by a culture. These relationships are a product of reading and writing practices; they enable writers and readers to make sense of a wide variety of texts by making use of a small range of techniques.

See also: code
conventions
genre
text

Intertextuality

Literature

To get you thinking

■ Of the following texts, which would you include in the category "literature"? (Put a check by your choices.)

☐ A car repair manual
☐ A novel by Charles Dickens
☐ A poem in *Playboy* magazine
☐ A joke you have been told
☐ A new comic book
☐ The first Superman comic

☐ A telephone book
☐ A Harlequin romance
☐ A poem in a poetry book
☐ A funny anecdote told by a professional storyteller
☐ A religious text

■ What factors have guided your selections?

Theory

Literature is notoriously difficult to define. Members of a culture usually "know" what counts as literature, even if they can't explain it. Prior to the eighteenth century, the English-speaking world used the term *literature* to refer to almost any kind of formal writing, from essays to poetry to scientific works. More recent usage has limited the term to "imaginative" or "fictional" works considered to be of value for moral, ethical, or spiritual reasons. This usage is neither consistent nor uncomplicated, however.

Decisions about what counts as literature tend to rely on two kinds of measures: formal or "technical" factors, and aesthetic or "value-based" factors. These measures are connected, of course. Formal or technical features are those which can be stated with fairly wide agreement. For example, "literary" works tend to feature invented characters and places, make systematic use of certain techniques such as narrative point of view or rhyme schemes, and follow certain conventional structures. (But a particular work might have all or none of these features.)

Aesthetic or value-based features are often less widely agreed on. These are measures of morality, beauty, or truthfulness which may be applied to a text. Because different groups of people may have different values and beliefs, there is often much disagreement at this level about what counts as literature. A Harlequin romance might fill many of the same technical requirements as a novel by Jane Austen, but some people argue that it is less skillful or less artistic and so is not "literature." Disagreements about literature often involve disagreements about whose values will win out.

One way of defining what counts as literature is to say that literature is what gets taught in literature classes. Educational institutions, along with publishing companies, play a powerful role in determining which texts will be taken "seriously" by people. This kind of definition recognizes that questions about literature are bound up with questions of social organization, power, and prestige. In any culture, those texts which count as literature tend to be the ones favored by the most powerful groups.

In modern Western cultures, what counts as literature is currently a matter of much debate. Many people are challenging the ability of ruling groups to define which texts are studied as literature. Thus literature has become a political issue.

Practice

Here are samples of the kind of exam questions which might have been asked of literature students in the past, and which might be asked now.

Traditional

- Shakespeare's plays are detailed studies in human nature. Discuss three of the human failings he explores, and show why his observations are still relevant today.
- *Pride and Prejudice*: a nineteenth-century Harlequin romance? Discuss the qualities in Austen's work which raise it above the standard of popular romance. Use references from the text to support your discussion.
- "The function of poetry is to offer a criticism of life which will sustain and console us"—Matthew Arnold. Explain Arnold's statement, with reference to two poets you have studied.
- Write a brief criticism of the following prose extract, commenting on the author's purpose, the techniques he employs, and the effectiveness of the writing.

Modern

■ All texts are constructed to offer a preferred reading. State the preferred reading offered by this poem, supporting your answer with detailed discussion of its structure and language. Conclude your discussion by suggesting who might support or reject the preferred reading.

■ The language and subject matter of Shakespeare's plays are shaped by contentious issues of the day. Discuss one clear example of this, making detailed reference to the text. Suggest two possible readings of the example which might be constructed by modern audiences.

■ The use of first-person point of view in Maxine Hong Kingston's novel *The Woman Warrior* enables Western readers to identify with the privileged position of the Chinese narrator. Show how this marginalizes the American characters in the novel, and discuss the effect of this with regard to constructions of race.

1. Following is a range of conflicting beliefs about literature. Decide whether each one is a "traditional" or "modern" assumption, based on the evidence of the sample examination questions printed above.

  ■ Literature is above differences of race, class, etc.   T   M
  ■ Literary texts contain fixed meanings.   T   M
  ■ Literary texts serve the interests of specific groups.   T   M
  ■ Literary texts are the expression of an author's
    thoughts and feelings.   T   M
  ■ Literary texts embody the highest human values.   T   M
  ■ Literary texts represent specific versions of reality.   T   M
  ■ Literary works "naturalize" social conflicts.   T   M

2. An interesting way of defining literature is to start by looking at how our culture signals to us that a work is "literature." How many signals can you add to this list?

  ■ The text is included in many literature courses.
  ■ The text is issued in expensive bindings, limited editions, or under special publishing imprints.
  ■ The text remains in print for a long time; often through a number of publishers.

■ The text is referred to—directly or indirectly—in other "literary" works.

■ The text is filed under the "800s" in libraries.

■ The text is written about in critical journals.

■ _____

■ _____

■ _____

■ _____

■ _____

■ _____

Are these signals used because a work is "literature"; or does it become literature because the signs are used? What do these signals tell us about how we are expected to approach literary texts as *readers*?

Summary

Literature refers to a shifting category of texts defined by a complex combination of factors including textual features and value judgments. The category of writing that we call literature is not self-evident but is produced by the interaction of various social institutions such as schools and the publishing industry.

See also: criticism
text

Literature

Marxist Criticism

To get you thinking

■ From your general knowledge of Marxism, which of the following things do you imagine Marxist critics might do with literary texts?

☐ Look for signs of Western decadence?
☐ Burn them?
☐ Worship them?
☐ Criticize them for promoting capitalism?
☐ Ban them from sale?
☐ See them as offering moral guidelines?
☐ Analyze the ideas they promote in society?
☐ Use them as communist propaganda?

Theory

The German philosopher Karl Marx argued that the way people think and behave in any society is determined by basic economic factors. In his view, those groups of people who owned and controlled major industries could exploit the rest of the population, first through conditions of employment, and second by forcing their own values and beliefs onto other social groups. Marxist criticism applies these arguments to the study of literary texts.

Marxist critics see literature as playing a role in this kind of exploitation. Their argument has two strands: first, they point out that literary works are commodities which can be bought and sold (and which can therefore be used to make a profit). Second, they argue that the reading and writing of literature is important in the spread of beliefs and values in a society. In other words, they see literature as a commodity which has certain social effects.

Marxist criticism approaches texts on a number of levels. On the one hand, the critic might explore the way different classes of people are represented in texts. For example, Marxist criticism might show us that a modern television drama focuses only on middle-class characters, thereby distorting the "true picture" of society, where many people are poor and homeless. This kind of criticism often argues for *social realism* in literature: a picture of society which accurately reflects class differences and differences of power.

On another level of analysis, Marxist criticism examines the particular form of a text. For example, it might argue that the sonnet, a poetic form which uses complex images and rhetoric, is a particularly middle-class form of writing, since it requires readers who are well educated (and therefore comparatively wealthy). In contrast, the realist novel, which relies on "straightforward" narrative, might be seen as requiring a less well educated readership. Marxist critics would use these observations to explain why it is that sonnets have traditionally been regarded as fine literature, whereas novels were initially regarded as trivial entertainments.

Marxist critics use these (and other) approaches to a text in order to challenge oppressive beliefs and values which might be promoted in certain texts and certain reading practices.

Practice

This extract is from the children's story *Peter Pan* by J. M. Barrie.

Mr. Darling used to boast to Wendy that her mother not only loved him but respected him. He was one of those deep ones who know about stocks and shares. Of course, no one really knows, but he quite seemed to know; and he often said stocks were up and shares were down in a way that would have made any woman respect him. Mrs. Darling was married in white, and at first she kept the books perfectly, almost gleefully, as if it were a game, not so much as a brussel sprout was missing; but by and by whole cauliflowers dropped out, and instead of them there were pictures of babies without faces. She drew them when she should have been toting up. . . . Mrs. Darling loved to have everything just so, and Mr. Darling had a passion for being exactly like his neighbors; so, of course, they had to have a nurse.

1. What assumptions might a young reader form from this text? (Check off your selections.)

   ☐ That "normal" people have servants (a nurse).
   ☐ That women respect men who know about money.
   ☐ That wealth is unequally distributed in society.
   ☐ To be different from others is shameful.
   ☐ Women should not have to be financially dependent on men.
   ☐ Women are unreliable employees as they are distracted by thoughts of motherhood.

2. Which of these two readings of *Peter Pan* would you support?

   ▪ It is an innocent story, told in terms of how the world looks to a child.
   ▪ It entertains its readers with a middle-class, British, male-oriented view of the world, but presents this way of thinking as amusingly typical.

3. If you were a parent, what action might you take with regard to *Peter Pan*?

   ▪ read it to children because it is entertaining?
   ▪ read it to children for fun, but discuss other possible readings?
   ▪ read other books which present alternative views of life?
   ▪ confiscate it and give children *Das Kapital* to read?

Summary

Marxist criticism examines the role played by literature in maintaining values and beliefs which support the ruling classes in a society. It explores both the features of the text, and the historical background in which the text is created, circulated, and read.

See also: class
          ideology

Marxist Criticism

Narrative

To get you thinking

Here is a list of words which begin with the letter H.

Hurry   Highway   Hitchhiker   Hurtle   Hospital

- Try reading the list as a kind of story.
- Is this merely a random list? Or are you able to read it as a story because it has been assembled as a kind of narrative?
- Test the effect of changing the order of the words. Does a different order still produce a "story"?
- What happens to the list when you approach it as a story? Do you find yourself doing any of the following:

  ☐ making connections to form a plot?
  ☐ "filling in" gaps?
  ☐ imagining a "character" to whom the story relates?
  ☐ imagining a person who is viewing or reporting events?

Theory

Narrative refers to the techniques and conventions by which a story is created. These include not only features of the text itself, but also certain conventions of reading. In most cases, textual features and conventions of reading dovetail together, so that the text seems to offer a "window onto the world," even if what we see through that window is a place or another time far removed from our own.

This impression of believability or *realism* is created by specific techniques and practices. These include processes of selection and organization. From the almost infinite possibilities of thought and action, texts offer a *selection* which conforms to certain limited beliefs and values. For example, we can recognize some familiar character "types" that appear in many stories: the loner, the man of action, the jealous woman, and so on. "Recognizing" such character types involves applying certain rules of reading in order to assemble textual elements in conventional ways. This has the effect of reinforcing prevailing prejudices about sexes, races, and classes.

The selected material is also *organized* in a specific way. In this process the basic *story*—a sequence of events following one after another, is arranged as a *plot*—a set of events structured to achieve an effect (for example, the use of flashback to create mystery). In addition, the story elements are conveyed to the reader by a storytelling voice, the narrator, which can take a number of forms. The narrator may be *"omniscient"*— able to report on the thoughts and actions of all characters; *limited*—able to report on some events only; or the narrator may be a character in the story (a *first-person* narrator.)

A great variety of texts use these techniques. Even television news bulletins (which are supposedly "factual" reports about the "real" world) select, organize, and narrate in this way. The concept of narrative therefore cuts across the traditional distinction between fiction and nonfiction texts. Because all texts necessarily select and organize material from a certain perspective, we can say that they are all fictional to some degree.

Practice

Because they are made from language, and because language is a medium of social struggle, texts always contain traces of social conflicts—between classes, races, sexes, and so on. In narratives, these conflicts are often resolved in favor of one side by the action of the narrative. Here is one thread of narrative from the science fiction movie, *The Abyss*.

> (1) Lindsay Brigman is a capable professional woman who designs submarine workstations for drilling rigs. She has separated from her husband due to career conflicts; she refuses to give up her career to be simply "Mrs. Brigman." Many of her co-workers dislike her; they think she is too "hard." (2) When the U.S. navy calls for assistance with a dangerous undersea mission, Lindsay is put in charge of a submarine station and its crew—including her estranged husband. (3) Lindsay and her husband must leave the station in a small sub to undertake a dangerous task. The sub is damaged, the air runs out, and they cannot get back to the station. (4) With only one scuba tank, Lindsay agrees to "drown" and let her husband take her back to the station by swimming, because he is the stronger swimmer. (5) On their return to the station, the husband revives Lindsay, literally bringing her back to life. In her weakened condition, she learns to depend on others for help. (6) The husband must then leave the station once more to undertake an even more dangerous task. He succeeds against incredible odds, partly due to Lindsay's encouragement over the intercom, and saves them all. (7)

Having worked together to complete the mission, the two rediscover their love. Lindsay wants to be "Mrs. Brigman" again, and the movie ends "happily."

This thread in the film's story clearly encodes the social debate over gender roles—whether a married woman should have the same opportunities as a married man. Like many narratives, this one involves a transformation (change) which resolves a conflict.

1. Which character undergoes the transformation? At what point in the story do you think this occurs?
2. The transformation is brought about by the issue of physical strength (who is the best swimmer). Does this support stereotyped views of masculinity and femininity in your culture?
3. Restructure the narrative of the film from point 4 to point 7, so that the man undergoes a transformation.

(4) _____
(5) _____
(6) _____
(7) _____

This shows how narrative itself can "resolve" conflicts that are not openly discussed in the language of the text.

Summary

Narrative refers to the techniques and processes by which stories are produced. These involve the selection and organization of textual material, and the operation of rules of reading which assemble that material in ways designed to resolve social dilemmas (often in favor of the dominant view).

See also: conventions
          point of view
          reading practices

Narrative

New Criticism

To get you thinking

New Criticism is an approach to literature which argues that meaning is produced by "the words on the page." It rejects any reference to the author's intentions or to any other factors "outside" the text.

■ Below are some possible sources of information that a critic might refer to when studying a text. Indicate whether each item of information might be accepted (A) or rejected (R) by a New Critical reader.

The opinions of the writer's friends and family.	A	R
A close reading of the text itself, with attention to word meanings and structure.	A	R
The historical circumstances in which it was written.	A	R
The beliefs, values, and practices of those who read it.	A	R
Evidence left by the writer (in the form of notes, letters, etc.)	A	R
Information about changes in the meaning of words over time, and from place to place.	A	R

■ What might be some advantages and disadvantages of approaching texts in this way?

Theory

The term *New Criticism* is given to the work of influential British and American critics of the 1940s and '50s. The New Critics argued that the meaning of literary works could be revealed only by concentrating on the text itself. In saying this, they were reacting against traditional forms of scholarship, which saw literary meaning as being a reflection of the author's thoughts, feelings, and experiences.

The New Critics developed techniques of "close reading" and "practical criticism" to explore the rich and complex meanings of literary works. They believed that "literary" language was different from everyday language in being more emotive and stimulating. Also, they argued that the language of literary works was "self-sufficient": that is, that language generated meaning through relationships within the text, rather than by referring to things in the "real" world. This meant that the meanings of literary texts could remain the same over long periods of time, even though the "real" world changed.

Many of these critics believed that Western society was in decay, and they argued that literary texts could help save the culture because it preserved human values and imposed some kind of order on human experience. They therefore placed a very high value on literature; in fact, some saw literature as a replacement for religion, which was in decline. By reading the best literature, they believed, people could make contact with the best thoughts and ideals, and could rediscover their "common humanity."

Modern theories see this search for unity and coherence as being politically unacceptable. In arguing that their method revealed the "true" meaning of literary works, the New Critics implied that other readers and other readings were wrong. This suggests a desire to reshape society in terms of the values and beliefs of one group of people. The New Critics also lacked an adequate theory of language. They failed to see that meaning is produced in the interaction between language users; it does not exist in words themselves.

The New Critical movement has been very influential, however; and its emphasis on detailed study of the language and structure of texts is now a feature of most critical approaches.

Practice

Here is a brief extract from Shakespeare's *Macbeth*. It is from the speech delivered when Macbeth hears that his wife is dead.

> . . . Out, out brief candle!
> Life's but a walking shadow, a poor player
> That struts and frets his hour upon the stage
> And then is heard no more. It is a tale
> Told by an idiot, full of sound and fury,
> Signifying nothing.

1. The New Critics placed great emphasis on the richness and ambiguity of literary language. For each of the following words in the extract, circle the meanings which can be seen as relevant to your reading of the text above. (You may wish to look ahead to the next activity before you do this.)

Brief	Shadow
of short duration	reflection
concise	slight trace
small	unfortunate
an undergarment	an unreal image
obscurity	a form of stitching

Poor	Player	Struts
needy	musician	bulges
humble	actor	swells
a ghost	athlete	walks pompously
bad	gambler	props up
	manipulator	

Frets	Stage
gnaws	theatrical platform
carves,	embosses
cuts	scene of action
worries	stopping place
irritates	scaffold flooring

2. Based on the word meanings outlined above, and constraints imposed by the text, indicate which of the following statements represent acceptable readings of the text.

    ◾ Life is meaningless, like a fictional play.
    ◾ Life has meaning in itself: it does not signify (point to) something else.
    ◾ Death is the final end to a pointless existence.
    ◾ Earthly life is but a reflection of some deeper reality, therefore death is not a final end to existence.
    ◾ The lives people live are meaningful, even though people themselves do not know the meaning, like the idiot who does not know the meaning of his tale.

(In making your selections, did you assume that the various meanings should "fit together" and form a "whole"? Did you reject contradictory meanings? This way of reading is founded upon the New Critical idea that poems are autonomous wholes. It is an idea that has been challenged by more recent theory.)

3. This text is, of course, part of a speech to be delivered on stage by a player. This means that it is paradoxical (self-contradictory). It seems to tell us a "truth" (that life, like drama is meaningless), but if drama is meaningless, how can we accept this observation as a truth? Is this a dilemma we face in all studies of literature?

Summary

New Criticism refers to a method of literary study which emphasizes the "close reading" of texts without direct reference to the social and historical differences among readers. The New Critics saw great literature as offering order and a set of values—things they believed were lacking in society.

See also: deconstruction
poststructuralism
structuralism

New Criticism

Point of View

To get you thinking

■ Here is the same event told in four different ways. Who is "telling" each story? (Some possible choices are listed after the stories.)

1. I came rushing in, late from lunch. The last thing I wanted was to deal with a problem student, but there was Nigel Smith, looking like a condemned man. Suddenly I was fed up with being a principal. I wanted a vacation.

   Storyteller:

2. The principal entered his office on the run. He had the look of a man thoroughly fed up with life. When he saw the scruffy boy waiting in the corner, a look of pained displeasure came over him, and he sighed.

   Storyteller:

3. The principal rushed in. What a morning, he thought. I've got to get away for a while. Nigel Smith saw that this was not going to be a pleasant visit. Why did I have to pick today to punch Kevin Riley, he wondered.

   Storyteller:

4. You sit patiently, waiting, regretting. You see the principal rush in. He looks annoyed. You think to yourself, oh no, this is going to be horrible!

   Storyteller:

Here are some choices:

the principal; the principal's assistant; a female student; Nigel Smith; a mind-reading observer.

Theory

In this activity, you have been identifying the *narrator*—the imaginary "person" who seems to report the details of a story. This person doesn't really exist, of course. She or he is merely an effect of the way we assemble and read a collection of sentences. This imaginary person is our source of information about events and characters in the imaginary world of the story.

The narrator may be related to the imaginary world in different ways. This relation is called the *point of view*. She or he may be an "all-knowing" observer, able to report the reasons for each character's thoughts and actions: "He hated this job." This is called the *third-person omniscient* point of view (omni=all, scientia=knowledge). Or she may be able to report only actions, without knowing their cause: "He appeared to hate his job." This is called the *third-person limited* point of view. Or she may be someone who lives in the imagined world and reports her own observations and thoughts: "I sensed that he was fed up, but there was nothing I could do." This is called the *first-person* point of view. Other combinations are possible.

The point of view offered by a text can have a powerful influence on the reading process. For example:

■ Go back to the opening activity and see if you can correctly label the point of view used in each example.
■ Which version/s of the story seem(s) most neutral and objective, most authoritative?
■ Which version/s seem(s) to invite you into the "emotional life" of the characters?

Most texts maintain the same point of view throughout a story. This approach gives an impression of realism, because individual readers are used to viewing the world from one point of view—their own. Consistent point of view enables the values of one character to be emphasized or privileged at the expense of others, and so limits the range of meanings a reader can produce with the text. We therefore need to ask which values and interests a text is promoting through the use of a consistent point of view.

Practice

Here are some variations on an extract from Raymond Chandler's detective novel *The Big Sleep*. Here private detective Philip Marlowe confronts Joe Brody and a woman named Agnes, who he suspects of being involved in blackmail and racketeering.

1. Chandler's text. Consistent first-person point of view.

   . . . the door buzzer rang and kept on ringing. [Brody] didn't like that. I didn't like it either. If it was the police, I was caught with nothing to give them but a smile and promise. The blonde didn't like it. Nerve tension made her face old and ugly. Watching me, Brody jerked a small drawer in the desk and picked a bone-handled automatic out of it. He held it at the blonde. She slid over next to him and took it, shaking. "Sit down next to him," Brody said. "Hold it on him low down, away from the door. If he gets funny, use your own judgment. We ain't licked yet baby." "Oh, Joe," the blonde wailed. She came over and sat next to me on the davenport and pointed the gun at my leg artery.

2. Variation. Consistent third-person omniscient point of view.

   . . . the door buzzer rang and kept on ringing. Three hearts jumped. Brody didn't like it. Things were suddenly out of control. Marlowe didn't like it either. If it's the police, he thought, I've got nothing for them but a smile and a promise. The blonde didn't like it either. Nerve tension made her face old and ugly. She wanted to get away, anywhere. Watching Marlow, Brody jerked a small drawer in the desk. . . .

3. Variation. Variable or indeterminate point of view.

   . . . the door buzzer rang and kept on ringing. I didn't like it. If it was the police, I was caught with nothing to give them but a smile and promise. The blonde didn't like it. Nerve tension made her face old and ugly. Watching me, Brody jerked a small drawer in the desk and picked a gun out of it. He held it out to the blonde. He held it out to me. I didn't like it, the buzzer ringing like that. I didn't know what to do, wanted to get away. I saw Joe take a gun from the drawer. He held it out to me, a white handle, told me to cover the guy. I slid over to him and took it, shaking. Oh, Joe. I didn't know where to point it. Aimed at his leg. Marlowe was worried, and that got me worried. I didn't like it: too complicated all of a sudden. I found the bone-handled automatic in the drawer, handed it to Agnes. Sit down next to him. Hold it on him low down, away from the door. If he gets funny, use your own judgment. We ain't licked yet baby. She slid over to me and took it. She came over and sat next to me on the davenport and pointed the gun at my leg artery.

Write the number of the appropriate extract in the space provided.

Which extract:

- invites the reader to share the observations of a single character? _____
- requires the most effort on the part of the reader, to make sense of the story? _____
- requires the least effort, and seems the most "natural" way of telling the story? _____
- is most offensive to women (e.g., through the portrayal of Agnes)? _____
- is most effective at ignoring the concerns represented by "minor" characters? _____
- seems to remove the distinction between major and minor characters? _____

Which of these points of view is used most often in the stories you read? Which is never or rarely used? Can you suggest reasons for this?

Summary

Narrative *point of view* describes the imaginary relation between the narrator of a story, and the characters and events created by the narrative. It is an effect produced by conventions of reading and writing, and is used to "frame" a certain view of the world.

See also: narrative
writing and speech

Point of View

Polysemy

To get you thinking

■ Can you think of a single word that has all of the following meanings?

   1. Meanings: manual worker; skill; writing style; pointer on a clock; fixed quantity of certain fruits; applause; measure equivalent to four inches.

   Word:

   2. Meanings: fruit of a cereal crop; small particle; small unit of weight: 1/480 oz.; dye; texture; direction or intent; line of cleavage in stone.

   Word:

■ If single words can have so many potential meanings, how is it that language users can ever agree on the meaning of a text?

Theory

All of the signs which human beings use to communicate—including words and images—have the potential to mean more than one thing. This is called *polysemy* (from the Greek, poly=many, semeion=sign). The easiest way to get some sense of this potential for meaning is to look words up in a dictionary, where an attempt has been made to list a wide range of possible uses.

   In daily life, the context of a word or phrase often clarifies its meaning. The phrase "That's nice piping," is potentially ambiguous, since piping can mean: playing a musical pipe; squeezing decorative icing onto a cake; a length of conduit for transporting water; or cord-like ornamentation on clothing. But when the phrase is spoken to one bagpipe player by another, this ambiguity goes unnoticed.

Some words and phrases do cause problems, however. Phrases like "the history of early *man*" and "this is a *black* day for us all" are offensive to certain groups on grounds of sex and race. These terms may seem neutral and innocent to some people; their meaning may seem fixed and obvious. But others object to the associated meanings of these words: that "black," for example, is equated with "bad" in the expression quoted above. Where beliefs and values are concerned, pinning down the meaning of a word can depend not only on its possible meanings and the context in which it is used, but on the power and position of the people who use it.

For example, a government official and a group of protesters might both agree to this statement:

> In a democratic country we must respect people's rights.

But the crucial word *rights* may have different meaning in the language, or discourse, of each group.

This might be the government official's definition:

> Rights = freedoms granted to all citizens under national legislation and international law.

This might be the protesters' definition:

> Rights = basic freedoms which all human beings share and which governments are established to protect.

One side views rights as privileges given to people by a government; the other sees rights as freedoms which exist *before* the law, and which the law is called upon to protect.

In the reading of literary texts, some approaches emphasize the play of possibilities produced by polysemic language. Others place various limits on the meanings of a text. The meanings may be limited by appeals to: the author's intention; the surrounding context; the social circumstances in which the text operates, or a combination of these.

Practice

Shakespeare's Sonnet Number 73 is a richly polysemic text. It is possible to read the sonnet in at least five ways:

i.   as a series of metaphors about time, age, and the speaker's approaching death;
ii. as a protest against common attitudes to age and death;
iii. as a rejection of Christian philosophies of death;
iv. as a comment on the decline of the Christian church;
v.   as a series of metaphors about gaining immortality through art (poetry).

Here is the opening quatrain of the poem. (The complete poem is printed on page 90.)

> That time of year thou may'st in me behold
> When yellow leaves, or none, or few do hang
> Upon those boughs which shake against the cold
> Bare ruined choirs, where late the sweet birds sang.

1. Which of the following are possible readings of the various phrases in the opening quatrain? (Put a check by your choices.)

☐ "time of year" = time of life
☐ "time of year" = period of history
☐ "yellow leaves" = autumn
☐ "yellow leaves" = old pages of writing
☐ "boughs" = branches
☐ "boughs" = human limbs
☐ "shake against" = shiver
☐ "shake against" = protest/refuse
☐ "shake against" = be under threat
☐ "the cold" = indifference
☐ "the cold" = rejection
☐ "the cold" = old age
☐ "ruined choirs" = failing voice
☐ "ruined choirs" = choirstalls of ruined churches

Poststructuralist theory (so called because it follows on from structuralist principles but also questions them) argues that such standards are always *produced* by cultures in the first place, and that they operate in the interests of a particular section of society. This does not mean that the people in charge of such knowledges are deceitful and evil, or are involved in a huge conspiracy. Instead, it means that the way society is organized—through institutions such as the state, the family, the education system, the church, the media—shapes the way people view the world. In this way, particular systems of thought determine what will count as "knowledge" or "truth" in a particular place and time.

"Knowledge" about literature is produced in this way. Such knowledge is assembled and circulated within a collection of institutions: the university; the school; the publishing industry; the bookstore; the library. These institutions determine which books will count as literature, which people have the authority to speak about literature, and what kind of things can be said. And they justify the knowledge that is produced by referring to various sources of truth: the author's mind, or the "words on the page," or "real life." But all of this knowledge is "constructed"; it isn't natural and it isn't absolutely true.

Poststructuralism investigates these social structures and seeks to analyze how their knowledges and truths are constructed. In this way, it aims to show that knowledges which seem impartial and obvious can actually work in favor of some groups of people and against others—without people being conscious of this at all. When this approach is applied to literary texts, it is often called *deconstruction*.

Practice

Poststructuralism argues that what counts as "truth" or knowledge is produced by social *institutions*—organizational structures which shape the way people think and behave.

1. What are some of the institutions which shape the social meanings of the following subjects? (Each item is affected by more than one institution.)

You may find it helpful to choose from the following key institutions: religion; the media; the family; education; the military; the police; the prison system; the law; publishing; marriage; science; medicine; "common sense"; advertising; the mass media; consumerism.

Subject	Institutions
Literature	
Masculinity	
Criminality	
Intelligence	
Childhood	

2. In the left-hand column below are some "truth statements" produced by particular social institutions and forms of knowledge. In the right-hand column, try to suggest institutions/knowledges within which the statement might be regarded as true.

Statement	Institutions/knowledges
Madness results from the re-emergence of repressed mental traumas.	psychiatry/medicine
Madness is the condition of being possessed by evil spirits.	
Economic growth is the basis of a healthy society.	
The desire for economic growth is crippling the environment.	
The only effective way of dealing with young offenders is to punish them.	
The only way to deal with young offenders is to improve their living conditions and provide them with jobs.	

Whose interests might be harmed by each of the statements/knowledges in this list? Whose interests seem to be protected?

3. List some of the "truth statements" you have learned about literature (include some from this glossary!).

Statements

- Literary works have definite meanings.
- Literary works have shifting meanings.
- Literary works are universal.
-
-
-
-
-
-
-

Whose interests are served by the literary-critical knowledges these statements support?

Summary

Poststructuralism is a theoretical position which investigates the connections between systems of meaning/action and relations of power. It investigates how knowledges and "truths" are constructed, and how these serve particular interests. This theory has become known as poststructuralism because it follows on from structuralist principles, but also questions them.

See also: deconstruction
power
structuralism

Poststructuralism

Power

To get you thinking

■ Who is likely to be most "in charge" of the following situations?

A male doctor and a male patient discussing treatment for the patient's serious illness.

Two male mechanics justifying a car repair bill to the vehicle's owner—a female doctor.

A male mechanic trying to arrange a loan from a male bank manager.

■ How is the balance of power in these situations determined? By purely individual factors (e.g., one person's specialized knowledge) or by relations produced through social factors?

Theory

People commonly think of power as something that comes "from above": from the government, from the police, and so on. But we are all involved in relations of power whenever we deal with other people. Children and parents; wives and husbands; homosexuals and heterosexuals; women and men; teachers and students: interactions between all these people involve differences of power.

Power is an effect of unequal relations between people that society recognizes as belonging to certain groups. Social practices sort people into a variety of groups. These groups may be based on class (employers, employees), gender (women, men), sexuality (straight, gay), age, profession, and so on. These groupings arise from the basic organization of a society. A capitalist society, for example, creates the categories of boss and worker, and produces the power differences between them. A communist society creates the categories of "party member" and "nonmember."

Because power is an effect of social structure, and not an absolute force imposed from above, nobody is completely powerful or powerless. But people have different degrees of power, depending upon how they are "located" in society. Through practices such as reading and writing, the members of different groups interact. In the course of this interaction alliances and oppositions are formed. These complex alliances form a *hegemony*—a network of social groups which "work together" in an unequal partnership against other groups.

The issue of power is crucially important to any study of literature and communication, because reading and writing are practices through which different groups promote their views of the world.

Practice

The following extract is from the short story "Listen to the End" by Tony Hunter. The story is an extended description of a woman who comes home to her apartment and gradually develops the impression that some-one else is there watching her. It could be read as a mystery or suspense story.

> As she turned, an impression, a feeling so intense that it flashed across her mind with the clarity of a neon sign, of not being alone, stopped her movement. The hairs prickled on the nape of her neck and so certain was the feeling that she was being observed that, in an unconscious gesture of femininity she folded one arm across her breasts while the other hand dropped to her belly. The feeling, which lasted perhaps a millisecond, was so strong that for that moment she knew that if she had turned a fraction quicker, she would have glimpsed the face of her observer. Still she stood for a second more, frozen in naked vulnerability while her heart thudded against her chest. [The story continues in this vein, with frequent and detailed descriptions of the woman's naked body and her fear.]

Perhaps the most disturbing feature of this story is the amount of infor-mation the text does *not* have to include. Most readers use a host of unconscious assumptions about men and women to fill "gaps" in the story. The structure of the story invites this gap filling because it repro-duces a *power relation* we are already familiar with.

1. Which of the following assumptions did you read into the story? For each one, indicate whether the information is supplied by the story (S) or the reader (R).

	S	R
The woman is young and attractive.		
The hidden observer is a man.		
The woman is in danger.		
Men "naturally" prey on women.		
The threat is partly or entirely a threat of sexual violence.		

2. How closely can the story be argued to match up with social structures of gender and power?

   ■ Which sex is "looked at" the most?
   ■ Which sex does most of the looking?
   ■ Which sex is assumed to be most vulnerable?

3. Which of the following features of the text reproduce the social power relations of gender and sexuality? Rank these features from most important to least important.

Textual Features	Ranking
Descriptions of the woman's body and her reactions.	
The point of view, which "exposes" the woman to view but offers no comment on the hidden intruder.	
The conventional plot: someone being followed, watched or overheard by a person or thing she or he cannot see.	
The vocabulary.	

4. This story invites readers to take up the position of the hidden intruder, which is a position of power structured by social assumptions about men and women. The story positions its readers as heterosexual males. But what of women readers? How do they "fit into" the story?

Summary

Power refers to the ability of members of one group to exert influence (even unconsciously) over members of another group due to socially constructed differences between them. Literary texts can be examined and judged in terms of whether they reproduce or disrupt power relations.

See also: class
          gender
          feminist criticism
          Marxist criticism

Power

Psychoanalytic Criticism

To get you thinking

■ Can you match up these common literary symbols with their supposed unconscious meanings?

Symbol	Unconscious Meaning
Houses/buildings	Birth
Small animals	Male genitals
Giants	Female genitals
Bushes/woodland	The self
Snakes	Parents
Water	Brothers & sisters

Theory

Psychoanalysis is a theory of mental operations developed by Sigmund Freud but more recently extended by theorists such as Jacques Lacan. Where Freud concentrated on the unconscious life of individuals, later theorists have explored the way language and culture provide an unconscious dimension to social life.

Popular conceptions of psychoanalytic criticism see it as a way of "decoding" the sexual symbolism of literary texts in order to uncover the author's unconscious obsessions. This is a distortion of the method because it fails to recognize that literature is a public medium. The symbols in literary texts generally represent the *culture's* obsessions. Images of snakes in a story do not express the author's personal preoccupation with the male genitals; but they may reflect a *cultural* preoccupation with images of male power, as encoded in language and other social practices.

Modern psychoanalytic criticism offers a method of textual analysis which explores the relationship between cultural processes and the construction of personal identity. According to this model, infant children pass through three stages in their progress toward selfhood.

■ The "Real" (0–6 months):

In this first stage, children are unaware of any distinction between their own bodies and the world around them; they are merged with an "oceanic" world.

■ The "Imaginary" (6–12 months):

In the second stage, children become aware of their separation from the world, and form a primitive sense of self by "borrowing" identity from other figures, such as parents. This is a stage where the child confuses its identity, sometimes imagining itself to be someone else.

■ The "Symbolic" (12–18 months):

Finally, at the age when they acquire language, children become aware of the differences between "self" and "others." By this stage, social influences have shaped the minds of boys and girls differently, so that boys are argued to have become active, competitive, and domineering, whereas girls are said to have become passive, cooperative, and submissive.

Psychoanalytic criticism sees literary texts as the culture's "unconscious" retelling of this development. For this reason, psychoanalysis is used by some feminist critics, because it illustrates the role played by literature in observing and reproducing differences between the sexes. This kind of analysis examines the way in which personal identity is produced as an effect of one's relations with other people. An important concept is *mirroring*—the process of producing an identity by identifying with someone else's position. This concept can be applied to the analysis of character relationships, and also to readers, who may identify with the characters in a story.

Practice

Here is a general summary of the plot of *Star Wars*, a popular science fiction movie.

> Luke Skywalker lives on a farm with his adopted parents. He knows nothing of his real family, and he dreams of adventure. • One day, Luke meets an old man who tells him of his dead father, a great warrior who fought against the evil Empire which now rules the galaxy. • Luke vows to become a warrior like his father, and to defeat the evil Emperor. • In the course of his adventures, Luke rescues Princess Leia. He competes with a friend, Han Solo, for her affections. • Luke learns that his father is not dead after all, but has turned to evil and is one of the Emperor's strongest supporters. Furthermore, he finds that Leia is his sister. • Luke must face his father in order to defeat the Emperor. Luke succeeds in rescuing his father from the Emperor's evil influence. Together they win the final battle, but Luke's father dies. • Luke finds satisfaction, at last knowing who he is, and taking his place in the world.

Like many stories, this one can be read as retelling the story of identity formation. The story follows the main character's move from "obscurity" (farm life) through "identity confusion" (who is his real father? who is his sister? is he like his "good" father or his "bad" father?) to "independence." But, as feminist critics point out, this is the story of the *male's* development. The only female character in the story (the Princess) does not grow and develop—she is merely the prize which the male characters compete for (and which both characters win—one as sister, one as lover!).

Psychoanalytic criticism often explores how readers read these male-oriented narratives, and how this reinforces the reader's gender identity.

1. Which of the following, do you think, are the most likely reading patterns for male and female viewers of *Star Wars*? Indicate whether each reading seems likely (L) or unlikely (U).

▮ Males will identify with Luke and imagine themselves as heroic figures. _____

▮ Females will identify with the hero's position, and temporarily "forget" their femininity. _____

▮ Females will identify with the Princess and enjoy the romance of being rescued and fought over by dashing young men. _____

▮ Males will identify with the Princess and temporarily "forget" their masculinity. _____

Do any of these choices challenge the gender identities offered by the film?

2. Which psychoanalytic stage does the reader seem to re-enter when viewing a film or reading a story: the real, the imaginary, or the symbolic? Why?

Summary

Psychoanalytic criticism sees literary texts as representing the unconscious thoughts and desires shared by members of a culture. It provides a way of exploring the social construction of personal identities, especially through the reader's interaction with the text.

See also: feminist criticism
identification

Psychoanalytic
Criticism

Race

To get you thinking

■ Western science recognizes roughly ten "geographical" races. These are based on minute differences, such as blood types, between geographical populations. Do you know which of the following categories you belong to? (Circle your selection.)

Capoid	Congoid	Caucasoid	Indic
Mongoloid	Australoid	Polynesian	Melanesian
Micronesion	Amerindian		

■ These categories are unfamiliar to many people. Categories such as "black" and "white" are much more familiar and powerful. Why should this be?

Theory

The concept of race is used to divide people into groups on the basis of certain arbitrarily selected hereditary characteristics. The concept of race works to emphasize, explain, and excuse the power of some groups over others. By drawing attention to noticeable but meaningless differences, such as skin color, social practices *construct* racial categories. This then enables members of one "race" to argue that "other" races are naturally inferior and so must be controlled. The concept of race is therefore tied to differences of power between groups of people.

Questions of race are relevant in literature study because literary texts, and readings of them, play a role in constructing images of race. Such images are often inaccurate and limited, and serve only as "negative images" against which the dominant culture can define itself. In fact, dominant cultures often do not see themselves as members of a race, but as "ordinary people." They see themselves as a normal standard against which other races can be judged. For this reason, the texts produced by dominant groups tend to either *ignore* racial and cultural differences (a way of making other races "disappear") or emphasize and criticize such differences.

Dominant representations of race are often promoted so powerfully that they come to be regarded as "true," even though they may be both inaccurate and unjust. When such images become "official" in schools and the media, they can shape the thinking of *all* groups.

In the study of texts, we need to explore constructions of race, asking who is in control of the text, whose values are being promoted, and whose interests are being served by representations of race.

Practice

This short extract is from Herman Melville's novel, *Moby-Dick*. Written almost 150 years ago, the book constructs "race" in terms that are now considered offensive and unacceptable. Here the narrator describes a fellow sailor, a heavily tattooed man called Queequeg.

> With much interest I sat watching him. Savage though he was, and hideously marred about the face—at least to my taste—his countenance yet had a something in it which was by no means disagreeable. You cannot hide the soul. Through all his earthly tattooings, I thought I saw the traces of a simple, honest heart; and in his large, deep eyes, fiery black and bold, there seemed token of spirit that would dare a thousand devils. And besides all this, there was a certain lofty bearing about the Pagan, which even his uncouthness could not altogether maim. He looked like a man who had never cringed and never had a creditor. Whether it was, too, that his head being shaved, his forehead was drawn out in freer and brighter relief, and looked more expansive than it otherwise would, this I will not venture to decide; but certain it was that his head was phrenologically an excellent one. It may seem ridiculous, but it reminded me of General Washington's head, as seen in the popular busts of him. Queequeg was George Washington cannibalistically developed.

1. In this portrayal, Queequeg's "differences" are treated as surface features. The passage suggests that "underneath" the man is a "normal" human, and perhaps a noble one. Find references to his "savagery" and his "civilized humanity."

"Savagery"	"Civilized humanity"
tattooed face	simple, honest heart

Which details make Queequeg acceptable to the narrator: their respective "differences" or their "similarities"?

2. Some phrases in the passage can be read as expressing the narrator's surprise at how civilized this "cannibal" is. Underline these sections (for example, "it may seem ridiculous . . .").

3. Here are three possible readings of the passage which account for the narrator's surprise in terms which now are read as racist.

- ■ Queequeg is unusual in being more civilized than others of his race.
- ■ All people of Queequeg's race, although superficially strange, are just like the narrator, deep down.
- ■ Queequeg's primitiveness reveals an honest humanity which the narrator's people have lost touch with.

In *all* of these readings the behaviors and beliefs of Queequeg's own culture are ignored in favor of the narrator's beliefs and values. Queequeg's culture is made *meaningless*.

Which of the following approaches might have produced a fairer description of cultural differences? Rank the possibilities.

Approaches	Ranking
Explaining Queequeg's appearance in terms of his own culture?	
Explaining the narrator's appearance in terms of his own culture?	
Providing a detailed description of Queequeg without comparison or comment?	
Including a similar account from Queequeg's point of view, describing the narrator?	
Including details of things the narrator did not like about Queequeg?	

Make a note of any problems with each approach in terms of both the textual features and reading practices which might be involved. (For example, might a particular reading practice still produce readings of Queequeg as "strange" and the narrator as "normal" despite changes to the point of view?)

Summary

Race refers to a category of *cultural* difference which is explained in terms of biology or heredity. Textual representations play a role in constructing "race" as a "natural" category. Such representations generally serve the interests of dominant groups by defining other "races" as abnormal.

See also: feminist criticism
         reading practices
         representation

Race

Reading Practices

To get you thinking

■ Each of these four puzzles represents a common word, phrase, or popular saying. Can you work them out?

A   B   C   D

■ When you have the answer, try stating some "rules" that will tell people how to read this kind of puzzle.

Rules:

1. _____

2. _____

3. _____

Theory

Reading a literary text can be likened to the process of solving the puzzles printed above. Readers process the visual information provided to them by applying a set of rules. In the example above, some of the rules might be:

■ the placing of letters and words often represents a preposition (for example; below, above, between);

■ single letters often refer to words with the same sound (for example; I = eye); and so on.

The rules which readers apply to a text are not personal and unique. They are normally shared by members of a community. The application of a shared set of rules is known as a *reading practice*, and reading practices are the strategies by which readers make sense of a text. Because most of us learn these rules at an early age, and because we apply them to so many texts, we tend to forget that we are using a set of rules at all. Instead, reading comes to seem "natural." The process of reading is, however, quite complicated. In reading a literary text, readers commonly do all of the following:

- decode words and phrases according to dominant meanings;
- look for patterns of repetition and description, and interpret these as meaningful symbols or images;
- invent connections between words and phrases so as to build up a "complete" world from the limited details in the text;
- construct an imaginary speaker for the writing (the narrator);
- treat the characters as imaginary people whose thoughts and actions can be judged;
- pay attention to some features of the text and ignore others, using past reading experiences as a guide; and so on.

Because texts provide a very limited amount of material to work with, readers supplement the text with background information provided by the beliefs, values, and practices of their culture. In many cases, readers do this so well, and agree with one another so closely about their readings of a text, that the whole process seems perfectly natural and obvious. When this happens, we say that the readers are using a dominant or naturalized reading practice—one which "plays by the same rules" as the text.

However, some people may choose to work with a *resistant reading practice*—that is, a way of reading which changes the rules and works "against the grain" of the text. Resistant reading is a refusal to play by the conventional rules. Like an audience that heckles a bad magician by exposing his tricks, resistant readers challenge the text by taking a sceptical approach. Resistant reading means refusing to accept the illusion that the text has an obvious meaning, or that it is complete and whole. Instead, it focuses on the gaps, silences, and contradictions which are present in all texts. The aim of resistance is usually to highlight beliefs and values which would be taken for granted in a dominant reading.

Practice

Here is an extract from *Heart of Darkness* by Joseph Conrad. It is part of the story narrated by Marlow, a sailor, who tells of his adventures in Africa.

> Now when I was a little chap I had a passion for maps. I would look for hours at South America, or Africa, or Australia, and lose myself in all the glories of exploration. At that time there were many blank spaces on the earth, and when I saw one that looked particularly inviting on a map (but they all look that) I would put my finger on it and say, When I grow up I will go there. The North Pole was one of these places, I remember. Well I haven't been there yet, and shall not try now. The glamour's off. But there was one yet—the biggest, the most blank, so to speak—that I had a hankering after.

Following are two very different readings of the extract, produced by two critics.

> 1. Conrad has given us an image from his own childhood—the blank map, waiting to be filled in—as a window onto Marlow's character, and a figure which draws us to him through the human spirit of adventure. For Marlow is the adventurer in all of us, and it is the timeless lure of the unexplored that makes a sea story so fascinating. Charlie Marlow, while unique and individual, represents the brave men of all ages—Columbus, Marco Polo, James T. Kirk—whose exploits touch something deep within us all.

> 2. *Heart of Darkness* reproduces the values of European imperialism. Those "blank spaces" were never blank; they were filled with people who the European powers simply chose to ignore. This "blankness" is the myth which all colonial powers promote to excuse their invasions. The book also reproduces masculine fantasies of domination. The "civilizing" of "primitive" cultures, like the "taming" of wives is all about imposing one's will to dominate others. It is no accident that "unexplored" continents are so often portrayed as mysterious "feminine" realms.

Each of these readings has been produced through a certain reading practice—a set of rules for making sense of the text.

1. Sort the following rules into two groups: those used by critic 1, and those used by critic 2.

- Read the text as the expression of the author's own ideas and experiences. _____
- Read the text as a comment about human nature. _____
- Read the text as evidence of struggles between different groups of people. _____
- Treat characters in the text as human beings, and identify with their experiences. _____
- Read the text's images as developing a theme or idea. _____
- Challenge the validity and acceptability of images in the text. _____
- Read the text as a patchwork of dominant cultural beliefs and values. _____
- Treat characters merely as devices used to develop ideas in the text. _____

2. Which of the critics seems to offer a dominant reading? Which offers a resistant reading?

Summary

Reading practices are the processes and cultural assumptions which readers use in making sense of a text. Different practices applied to the same text will produce different readings. The choice of one practice over another depends upon the reader's training, which is determined by social factors such as education, cultural background, and dominant *ideologies*.

See also: ideology
readings

Reading Practices

Readings

To get you thinking

■ Three people watching a football game have been asked to explain what this cultural activity means. They are a sociologist, a psychologist, and an art critic. What is each person's answer?

1. Football is a competition in which players strive to achieve certain goals within a set of limits established by the rules. It is a ritual which reminds the audience of social values such as individual effort and the importance of success.

   Who?

2. Football is a kind of dramatic narrative which aims to entertain the audience. It has heroes and villains, a story, and lots of action. Sport of this kind is a modern form of theater.

   Who?

3. Football is an acting-out of certain male anxieties. It is a socially acceptable way for grown men to play together and keep company without having their masculinity questioned. It also provides an outlet for repressed homosexual impulses.

   Who?

Theory

Any cultural "text"—from football to poetry to marriage ceremonies—can mean different things to different groups of people. This is not because we all have personal or individual opinions, but because different groups might read the text in different ways. These different ways or *practices* of reading produce ways of thinking about a text which we can call *readings*. In the activity above you have seen three different readings of a football game.

Readings are meanings which are constructed *for* a text; they are not extracted from it. The readings we construct for a text relate to the ways of thinking and acting that are made available to us by our culture, our social positions, our genders, our professions, and so on. Readers often assume that the meanings they make are merely "common sense." But what we call common sense is itself made up of readings about aspects of the world—readings which provide us with "ready-made" ways of thinking.

For any specific text, some readings will be common, others will be rare. We can suggest three classes of reading.

- Dominant or preferred readings—these are readings which the text is designed to favor, and which represent the beliefs and values which are most powerful in a culture.
- Alternative readings—these are readings which are less common but acceptable, because they do not challenge the dominant reading.
- Oppositional or resistant readings—these are readings which are unacceptable in terms of the dominant cultural beliefs, and which challenge prevailing views.

Dominant readings are vigorously promoted through institutions such as the media, the law, education, and business, and are given privileged status. Alternative and oppositional readings tend to be marginalized, which means they circulate among smaller or less powerful groups of people.

Practice

Printed below is a summary of a "romantic" fairy tale. Before you read it, however, think about the *dominant readings* of romance in your culture.

1. Circle the dominant "romantic" reading for each of the following.

True love:	is never fulfilled	
	wins out in the end	
	doesn't really exist	
Princes:	wealthy	shallow
	charming	well educated
	beautiful	boring

Princesses:	wealthy	beautiful
	tragic	well dressed
	intelligent	snobbish

Male desire:	a desire for beautiful women
	a desire for intelligent women
	a desire for children

Female desire:	a desire to be loved
	a desire to be married
	a desire to be independent

Now read the summary of "Cinderella" which follows.

Cinderella lives with three stepsisters who are jealous of her beauty and who will not let her out of the house. One day, news arrives that the prince is holding a fabulous ball. The three stepsisters all go to the ball, each hoping that the prince will fall in love with her. Cinderella is left at home, but her fairy godmother appears and magically provides her with beautiful clothes and a carriage so that she can go to the ball. The spell will last only until midnight. **Cinderella is the most beautiful woman at the ball, and the prince will dance only with her.** She rushes out of the ballroom on the stroke of twelve, however, leaving only a glass slipper behind. The prince keeps the slipper and searches the land looking for its owner. When he comes to the home of the three stepsisters, each tries to force her foot into the slipper, but fails. The prince does not recognise Cinderella in her rags, but she is permitted to try the shoe also. When it fits, she is again transformed. The prince pleads with Cinderella to marry him, and she does.

2. The story contains numerous "gaps." For example, the sentence which is in **bolder** type gives us two facts but does not state the link between them. Readers must fill this gap by supplying the appropriate romantic reading. Which of the readings below fills the gap? (Refer to your answers to activity number 1 if necessary.)

■ true love   ■ prince
■ male desire   ■ female desire

To construct a dominant (that is, romantic) reading for the story, readers supply dominant readings from their culture to fill gaps in the text.

3. Here are two readings of "Cinderella."

a. The story presents an ideal image of romantic love. It shows that true love will prevail no matter what the odds, and it encourages people to believe that dreams can come true. The story encourages an optimistic outlook on life.

b. The story is about the shallowness of men who judge women solely on the basis of physical attractiveness. A man who will marry a woman on the basis of a few hours dancing is likely to leave her just as quickly. No wonder most of the women in the story are bitter. This should be read as a cautionary tale against the idea of romantic love.

The first of these is a dominant reading; the second is a resistant or oppositional reading. Go back to activity number 1 and underline the readings which have been used in constructing the oppositional reading of the text. Does the oppositional reading also make use of "available" ways of thinking?

4. What happens if we rewrite the "Cinderella" story, filling in the gaps with the required readings of men, women, and romance? For example:

Cinderella was the most beautiful woman at the ball. The prince loved beautiful women and always wanted to be near them, so when he saw her he would dance with no one else.

How does this rewriting change the preferred reading of the prince?

5. Go back to the three readings of football at the beginning of this entry. Can you say which is the dominant, alternative, and oppositional reading of football?

Summary

Readings are the meanings produced when a reader applies a particular reading practice to make sense of a text or some other element in the culture. Readings can also be established "ways of thinking" about some aspect of the world.

See also: reading practices
         ideology

Readings

Representation

To get you thinking

■ What common object is suggested by all of the following?

A B C D

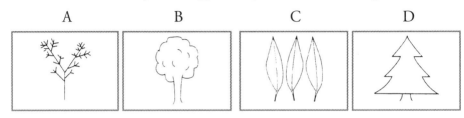

■ Is any of these images more "accurate" at signaling the concept "tree," or are they equally effective?
■ Do the images really look like real trees? Or could they easily stand for something else (e.g., a candle flame, an arrowhead)? What does this suggest about the signs and images we use to represent the world?

Theory

In everyday life we tend to think of texts as somehow "reflecting" the world around us. Some television programs seem to reflect the activities of "real" police, lawyers, and doctors. Some paintings seem to offer images of "real" trees and hills. Some novels and stories seem to offer reflections of "real" characters and events. These texts seem able to "call up" aspects of the world and present them to us. This process is called representation, which simply means to "present again."

New understandings of language and culture tell us that the representations we find in texts—these images of the world—are not reflections but *constructions*. That is, the images do not relate directly to an objective, "real world"; instead, they relate to habitual ways of thinking about and acting in the world. In other words, representations refer to *versions of reality* that particular cultures construct, and which people work within.

We can see an example of this in popular representations of men. Television and the movies repeatedly represent men in the roles of business executives, gunslingers, secret agents, explorers, and so on. These images rely on a narrow definition of masculinity: as active, ambitious, independent, and masterful. They reinforce popular ways of thinking about and being a man in Western culture. We know, of course, that most men can be cooperative, concerned, anxious, and uncertain. Representations which expand our idea of masculinity along these lines challenge popular thinking and might play a role in reshaping people's attitudes, values, and behaviors.

Representations cannot be judged on the basis of "accuracy." Instead, they must be evaluated in terms of their social effects. Some representations can be judged harmful and undesirable because they support a version of reality which favors some social groups and disadvantages others. Stereotyped representations of masculinity, for example, often present white, middle-class, heterosexual males as "typical." This ignores other forms of masculinity—that of gay men, for example.

Overworked or "formula" representations generally become *stereotypes*—simplified images which define certain groups of people in narrow ways. Examples of stereotypes would be the "dumb blonde" woman and the "strong silent" man.

Practice

The following "nonsense" poem is by Lewis Carroll.

Jabberwocky

Twas brillig, and the slithy toves
Did gyre and gimble in the wabe;
All mimsy were the borogoves,
And the mome raths outgrabe.

"Beware the Jabberwock, my son!
The jaws that bite, the claws that catch!
Beware the Jubjub bird, and shun
The frumious Bandersnatch!"

He took his vorpal sword in hand;
Long time the manxome foe he sought—
So rested he by the Tumtum tree,
And stood awhile in thought.

And, as in uffish thought he stood,
The Jabberwock, with eyes of flame,
Came whiffling through the tulgey wood,
And burbled as it came!

One, two! One, two! And through and through
The vorpal blade went snicker-snack!
He left it dead, and with its head
He came galumphing back.

"And hast thou slain the Jabberwock?
Come to my arms, my beamish boy!
O frabjous day! Callooh! Callay!"
He chortled in his joy.

'Twas brillig, and the slithy toves
Did gyre and gimble in the wabe;
All mimsy were the borogoves,
And the mome raths outgrabe.

1. How much of the poem's content refers to the reality of your everyday life? Put a check by anything which is part of your reality.

☐ Jabberwocks   ☐ tulgey woods   ☐ monsters
☐ fathers & sons   ☐ Tumtum trees   ☐ borogoves
☐ Bandersnatch   ☐ jaws and claws   ☐ Jubjub birds
☐ heroic adventure   ☐ vorpal swords   ☐ toves

The dominant reading of this poem produces it as an adventure in which a young man slays a monster. But where does this meaning come from, if not from a real world that is reflected in the story? The answer is that readers recognize the *structure* of the poem, which imitates the structure of popular stories about the heroic adventures of young men.

2. Which of the following best describes the structure of the poem?

a. Youth—challenge—mastery—maturity.
b. Introduction—development—climax—resolution.
c. Normality—disruption—heroism—normality.
d. Setting—plot—character—setting.

Of course, this is a trick question. All of these structures are bound together in the typical heroic narrative. Readers make meaning with the text by comparing it to other texts, not to their own experiences of the real world.

3. Through its structure, this poem calls up a set of conventional ideas about maleness and adventure. In this way, a particular *representation* of masculinity is produced. Which of the following are features of this representation? (Place a check by your choices.)

Masculinity =

☐ activity   ☐ aggression   ☐ emotion
☐ pride   ☐ individuality   ☐ dominance
☐ cooperativeness   ☐ fearfulness   ☐ bravery
☐ anxiety   ☐ sincerity   ☐ passivity

Is this a "dominant" or "alternative" representation of masculinity?

Summary

Representations are textual constructions which refer to habitual ways of thinking about or acting in the world. Although they seem to refer to the "real world," they actually refer to the cultural world which members of a society inhabit.

See also: class
           gender
           race

Representation

Semiotics

To get you thinking

■ Test your knowledge of the typical "Western" story. List three kinds of each of the following as they might occur in a Western story:

buildings			
costumes			
men			
social activities			
women			
locations			

■ Why does this narrow set of elements so often recur in Western stories?
■ What does this suggest about how such texts are produced?

Theory

Semiotics is the name given to a method of analyzing texts. Semiotic analysis sees a text as a collection of elements drawn from a social system of signs. Human beings use many kinds of sign-systems to communicate and make meaning. These include gestures, forms of dress, speech, writing, traffic signals, and so on. People make meanings by selecting elements from a system and combining these according to established rules. The elements which are selected are called *signs*, and the rules of combination are called *codes*.

When chefs create a menu, for example, they select a range of foods (for example, fish, meat, vegetables) and organize these into a sequential structure. Some items will be served together (for example, meat and vegetables), others will follow one after the other (for example, soup; then main meal; then ice cream). So, we can "read," a restaurant meal as a text assembled from a set of signs. We can also compare different texts: a vegetarian menu is different from a "standard" menu, and we can explain these differences in terms of the values and beliefs of different groups of people.

Semiotics approaches literary texts in much the same way. It explores the key signs in the text (for example, characters, places, actions, objects) and the ways in which they are combined (through structure and narrative). By exploring the social meaning of these selections and combinations, we can establish a relationship between the text and certain cultural beliefs and values. To be fully useful, this kind of analysis should also give some consideration to the different readings which might be produced from the text.

Practice

1. Here are some signs which might be found in a typical Western story. Can you add to the list?

black hats	white hats	outlaws	_____
stars	bibles	the town	_____
bar girl	law books	schoolmistress	_____

2. The signs in the text relate to powerful cultural beliefs. Circle the dominant beliefs which each of the following signs represents in your culture. (There may be more than one for each sign.)

White =	pure	dangerous	boring	good
Black =	dirty	evil	unlucky	exciting
Woman =	dynamic	passive	emotional	dependent
Man =	independent	powerful	rational	mysterious
Wilderness =	savagery	peace	refinement	progress
Town =	civilization	savagery	sterility	decline

3. The signs are related to one another in established ways. Which of the following are common features in a Western story?

The outlaws	a. come from outside the town.
	b. are members of the town.
The sheriff	a. is a loner.
	b. is a family man.
The townfolk	a. are friendly, church-going people.
	b. are unpleasant and selfish.
The written law	a. is stronger than the gun.
	b. is second to the "law of the west."

4. Many Westerns support conservative beliefs and values about men, women, the law, and "progress." Some of these are:

   ■ a man should be independent but not lawless;
   ■ men should follow a "natural law" when all else fails;
   ■ women and children (the family) represent civilization and must be protected by men;
   ■ community life should be regulated by forms of written law (for example, the biblical scriptures, judicial law).

Here are some different ways of selecting and combining signs in a Western. Which of the following would challenge these beliefs most powerfully? Indicate whether the change would be major, minor, or irrelevant (N/A).

	Major	Minor	N/A
The sheriff is a family man.			
The sheriff is a homosexual.			
The sheriff is black in a white town.			
The outlaw wins the gunfight.			
The sheriff wears black clothing.			
The schoolmistress shoots the villain.			
The outlaw is a woman.			
The sheriff is a woman.			
There is a trial instead of a shoot-out.			

How could each of these changes affect the meaning of the text for most people?

5. All of these are possible variations on the Western story, but they are rarely used. This is because the Western story is a text which supports certain beliefs about masculinity which cannot easily be challenged in our culture.

You might like to identify the signs, structure, and cultural function of some other common types of story, for example: the detective story; the romance; the police drama; the horror story. How are these texts constructed? What beliefs do they support?

Summary

Semiotics is the study of sign-systems and the way they operate within a culture. It examines texts not as "personal" messages sent by an author to a reader, but as collections of signs drawn from a public system of meaning, and representing certain cultural ideas.

See also: binary opposition
code
poststructuralism
structuralism

Semiotics

Structuralism

To get you thinking

■ You have been stopped in the street by a Martian linguist who wants to know how to make sense of the English language. She (it?) has collected the following set of words.

table	sat	red	on	happily	ran
a	dog	house	kicked	smooth	bright
slowly	under	over	soft	purple	soft
ball	John	Jane	bird	jumped	before
cup	carried	beside	in	gladly	the

■ Sort the words into different functional categories (e.g., naming words, action words, describing words, and others).

_____ _____ _____ _____ _____ _____

_____ _____ _____ _____ _____ _____

_____ _____ _____ _____ _____ _____

_____ _____ _____ _____ _____ _____

_____ _____ _____ _____ _____ _____

_____ _____ _____ _____ _____ _____

■ Now list some of the rules for combining these words in meaningful ways (e.g., describing words go in front of naming words). Hint: building some examples of right and wrong "sentences" from the jumble of words will suggest some rules.

Rules:

1. _____

2. _____

3. _____

4. _____

Theory

All cultural systems, such as language, are made up of a set of elements and a set of rules for combining these elements. This is true of gesture systems, fashion systems, and even systems of food and cooking. When we construct a sentence, or a meal, or when we get dressed in the morning, we select elements from the appropriate system, follow the rules for combining them, and produce a text which others in our culture will find meaningful. *Structuralism* is a method of analyzing the complex systems, or structures, which make these texts possible and meaningful.

The science of linguistics tries to describe a basic grammatical structure which makes all the sentences in a language possible. This means that linguistics can be a form of structural analysis. In the case of literature study, structuralist analysis has the same goal. It doesn't try to explain "the meaning" of texts; instead, it tries to demonstrate how texts are constructed, and how it is possible for them to mean.

A structuralist approach carves the text up into basic elements and then sets out to "discover" the rules by which these elements are related. Some rules may operate within a specific text, but others may be common to a great number of texts. For example, one structuralist study of myths argues that many mythic stories are constructed around three pairs of basic characters or "functions":

- Subject   (the person who is the focus of the narrative);
- Object   (the person, thing, or goal which defines the subject's task);
- Donor   (the person or thing which provides materials or information crucial to the subject's success);
- Receiver   (the person who receives the donor's gift or advice);
- Helper   (the person or thing which accompanies and assists the subject);
- Opponent (the person, thing, or place which stands in the way of the subject and must be overcome).

Note: a single character may have more than one of these functions; and some functions may be missing from some stories.

These basic functions relate to three aspects of narrative: desire, or aim; communication; helping or hindering. The film, *Star Wars* can easily be read in this way.

Luke Skywalker (subject) searches for his true identity in the form of his father and family (objects). Obi-wan Kenobi (donor) provides him with the necessary skill and information. C3PO and R2-D2 help Luke in his quest. Darth Vader (actually his father) and the Emperor oppose him. Luke finds both his father and his sister, Princess Leia (an "object" received by Luke as sister and by Han Solo as lover/wife).

Reading the text in this way enables us to see more clearly the relationship between *Star Wars* and many other epic stories, such as the Arthurian Legend and the story of Odysseus. In practice, however, we must consider not only how a text is constructed, but how it is *read*. Different groups of people may read the same story structure in different ways.

Practice

Here is a brief retelling of the story of Theseus and the Minotaur.

The people of Athens, defeated in battle by King Minos of Crete, must send a tribute of seven boys and seven girls to Crete once every nine years. These youths are fed to the Minotaur, a bull-like monster which lives inside a maze of stone. To end this slaughter, Theseus, son of the king of Athens, volunteers himself as a tribute, with the aim of slaying the Minotaur. Princess Ariadne, daughter of King Minos, falls in love with Theseus. She seeks the help of Daedalus, creator of the maze, who gives her a ball of thread and the secret of the maze. Theseus ties the thread to the entrance of the maze, enters the monster's lair, and slays it. He then retraces his steps by following the thread. Theseus returns to Athens with the young men and women he has saved.

1. Match the characters to the six functions:

Function	Character(s)
Subject (hero)	
Object(s)	
Donor	
Receiver	
Helper	
Opponent	

2. Give examples from the story which represent the following narrative elements:

Element	Example
A desire or goal	
Communication	
Help	
Hindrance	

3. Structuralism claims to make us conscious of rules and systems which are usually unconscious. The "narrative grammar" you have been working with can be expressed like this:

    A has a goal, or is given a task by **B**;
    C assists **A**;
    D opposes **A** and **C**;
    E perceives the solution to the task, and relays it to **A** or **C**;
    A achieves the goal or completes the task.

You can create plot outlines for your own stories by substituting specific characters and details into this basic formula. Try to produce two outlines as follows:

■ a "mythic" story using traditional characters and events (e.g., knights, princesses, dragons);
■ a modern "genre" narrative (for example, a science fiction story, Western, or horror story) using appropriate characters and events.

4. A study of narratives reveals that most subjects/heroes are male, whereas females tend to be objects or helpers. Is this required by the grammar of narrative? If not, how can you explain it?

Although it provides interesting perspectives in textual analysis, structuralism tends to disregard the role of *reading* in producing the meaning of a text. One might imagine, for example, that the people of Crete could produce quite a different reading of the Theseus myth. It is unlikely that they would read Theseus as a hero; he might not even be the main focus of the narrative for Cretan readers. The idea that narrative structures exist solely "in" the text must therefore be challenged.

Summary

Structuralism is a form of analysis which argues that an underlying system of elements and rules produces the meaning of a text. It downplays the role of individual authors by showing that texts are produced from the shared sign-systems of a culture.

See also: readings
reading practices

Structuralism

Style

To get you thinking

■ Do these four sentences all mean the same thing, or do their differences change the meaning significantly?

1. The sun rises red and gold behind the hills.

2. But look, the morn, in russet mantle clad,
   Walks o'er the dew of yon high eastward hill.

3. Bronze light spills from the rising sun and runs like furnace fire down the cool sides of the hills.

4. The earth turns and sweeps its geographic formations into the path of the sun's light, which, scattered and refracted by dust in the upper atmosphere, is shifted toward the red end of the spectrum.

■ Which of the passages seems most "literary" to you? Which seems the least literary? Rank them from 1 to 4 to indicate your choice.
■ What factors have you considered in making your decisions?

Theory

In literature study, *style* refers to the way textual elements (such as words, phrases, sentences, images) are organized in relation to one another. The point of examining style is to consider how it affects the meanings which readers make from the text.

The stylistic features in a text may be noticeable for a number of reasons, including *repetition* (repeated words or phrases, or repeated short sentences, for example), *contrast* (a short sentence coming after a series of long ones, or a simple everyday word in among a passage of complex vocabulary, for example), and *pattern* (a series of images which develop or elaborate a comparison, for example).

There are four basic dimensions of style.

- Word choice, or **diction**

  This refers to the type of words which dominate the text. The words may be taken from common speech, or from specialized vocabularies. They may represent the language of different social groups. They may be precise or ambiguous.

- Word order, or **syntax**

  Syntax refers to the ordering of elements in a sentence. Unusual word order often has significance for readers (compare "I cannot allow that!" with "That I cannot allow!"). In poetry, syntax is often manipulated to produce rhythms.

- **Rhetorical devices**, such as metaphor or simile.

  The use of metaphor, simile, symbol, personification, and other techniques may invite the reader to form particular associations, or to produce a wider range of readings from the text through ironic or ambiguous language. In *Hamlet*, for example, metaphors of disease and sickness may underscore the concept of corruption that is developed through the storyline.

- **Sentence organization**

  This includes the structure of sentences (simple, complex, periodic), their lengths, and various arrangements of these through repetition or patterning.

These stylistic features are not necessarily meaningful in themselves, however. We only notice them if they stand out within the codes of literary writing and reading that we employ. This means that different elements of style may be noticed by different readers at different times.

Practice

1. What are the notable stylistic features in each of the following passages? Choose from the following short descriptions.

   ■ inflated diction   ■ rhetorical devices (specify)
   ■ short sentences   ■ long sentences
   ■ syntax used for effect   ■ repetitive sentence structure

   A. The water shone pacifically; the sky, without a speck, was a benign immensity of unstained light; the very mist . . . was like a gauzy and radiant fabric, hung from the wooded rises inland, and draping the low shores in diaphanous folds. (Joseph Conrad, *Heart of Darkness*)

   Features:

   B. During the whole of a dull, dark and soundless day in the autumn of the year, when the clouds hung oppressively low in the heavens, I had been passing alone, on horseback, through a singularly dreary tract of country; and at length found myself as the shades of evening drew on, within view of the melancholy House of Usher. (Edgar Allan Poe, "The Fall of the House of Usher")

   Features:

   C. There were only two Americans stopping at the hotel. They did not know any of the people they passed on the stairs on their way to and from their room. Their room was on the second floor facing the sea. It also faced the public garden and the war monument. (Ernest Hemingway, "Cat in the Rain")

   Features:

   D. There was an inescapable sense of despair about the old school. It was there in the dying flowers which hung limp in the gardens; it was there in the muddy-colored carpets in the hallways; it was there in the shredded remains of the tennis nets which hung like the tattered rigging on some reef-wrecked sailing ship; and it was there in the people themselves who shuffled aimlessly down dark passages, spoke soundlessly in empty rooms, and sprawled awkwardly on the lawn like ancient insects trapped in amber. (Lorelei Parker, *School*)

   Features:

2. Which, if any, of the following effects might the styles of these passages produce? Match up the columns as you think best.

Possible Effects	Passage
Superiority and contempt	
Detached objectivity	
Seriousness/respect	
Apprehension	
Emotional emphasis	
Dreary boredom	
Exhilaration and delight	
Ironic amusement	

Would you have given different descriptions of the effects of the passages to those listed here? If so, list your own descriptions.

3. Stylistic effects are sometimes best demonstrated by substituting different words, phrases, or techniques for those used in the text. For example:

Passage A:

■ the sky . . . was a *benign immensity* of *unstained* light
■ the sky . . . was a *harmless expanse* of *clear* light
■ the sky . . . was a *peaceful area* of *blue* light

Try out the following changes and observe their effects.

■ change the sentencing in passage C by using punctuation and joining words (e.g., *and, but, also,* etc.);
■ remove all repetitions from passage D;
■ simplify the diction in passage A by replacing uncommon words with simple, everyday equivalents;
■ remove all adjectives, adverbs, and archaic expressions from passage B.

Summary

In literature study, *style* refers to the way textual elements are organized in relation to one another and in relation to the dominant codes of literary writing *and* reading. Attention to style is important because the organization of these elements can influence the way a text is read.

See also: figurative language
                imagery
                point of view

Style

Text

To get you thinking

■ Here is a list of techniques used in film texts. Can you state the meaning or significance of each?

Element	Meaning
The image gradually fades to black, then reappears.	Time has passed.
A low, rhythmic tone on the soundtrack.	
A woman's face is filmed in soft lighting.	
A figure is filmed from a low angle.	

■ How have these techniques come to convey their meanings?

Theory

Modern critical theory has vastly expanded the traditional concept of text. It argues that motion pictures, pop songs, novels, weddings, buildings, and more are all "textual." All of these things have the following features in common:

■ they are *material* objects or practices, not "ideas";
■ they are results of human activity, not natural phenomena;
■ they are made up of individual elements whose meaning depends upon their relation to other elements;
■ they make sense only within a system of meanings shared by a community of people.

For example, a motion picture consists of many small "meaning units" such as different camera angles, changes in lighting, styles of acting, sound effects, music, lines of dialogue, and so on. These units, or *signs*, make sense to viewers only because they are used in consistent ways within the text, and because they relate to similar signs in other motion pictures. This consistency gives rise to recognizable rules or *codes*. In the activity above you have identified parts of the *code* that governs the *signs* of a motion picture.

These same principles apply to social rituals such as weddings, and to literary forms such as the novel. Wedding ceremonies are built up from a system of public behaviors that includes gesturing, speaking, dressing, and moving. Novels are built up from the system of language, and from certain conventions of reading and writing. So, we can say that a text is any specific object or event constructed from the signs and codes of a social system of meaning.

Texts are always language-like in their operation. Their basic signs are like words; the rules they obey are like the grammar of a language; and their conventions are like familiar ways of speaking. Because these codes and conventions are built up through wide usage, a text gains its form and meaning through relation to other similar texts. This property is called *intertextuality*.

Intertextuality is not only a property of texts. It is also a feature of reading practices. Without the ability to apply similar rules to a variety of texts, reading would be impossible. We would have to learn a new set of codes, conventions, and reading practices for every work; that is, we would have to learn to read all over again every time we were confronted by a text. In order to "make sense" of a specific film, novel, or stage play, the reader must be able to apply a large body of knowledge and a range of techniques that is already familiar.

The meanings of a text are determined partly by the selection and arrangement of its signs, and partly by the way it is read. In a *closed text* the arrangement of signs in a text works to limit the number of possible readings. In an *open text* there is scope for many different readings to be produced. However, even in the case of an open text, powerful beliefs and values in a culture will normally encourage readers to produce only a narrow range of meanings for the text.

Practice

Here is a menu from an imaginary restaurant.

Soup: $5.00   *Entree:* $11.50

French Onion   Garlic Prawns
Pumpkin   Roman salad
Chicken   Ravioli

Main Meal:

Pan-fried fillet steak with red wine sauce $22.00
Roast pork medallions with bacon and sauteed mushrooms $18.00
Steamed dory fillets with cheese and shrimp sauce $20.00
Chicken breasts in filo, stuffed with pine nuts $18.00
Mushroom and tomato cannelloni $16.00

Your choice of:

Green salad: lettuces, peppers, celery, and fresh herbs
Fresh vegetables: potato, marrow, squash, carrot $5.00

Desserts: $6.00

Chocolate mousse   Special ice cream
Fresh fruits   Black forest gateau

Beverages:
Soft drinks   Tea   Wines   Coffee

We can think of the menu as a system of signs and rules from which people can construct a text: in this case, a four-course meal. The menu provides a reservoir of possibilities which may be realized in a variety of ways. However, any meal constructed from the menu will be shaped by the same set of signs and rules.

1. Break down the menu into its component signs (basic elements). There are three categories of sign: foods, cooking methods, and accompaniments. (These are like the basic elements of a language: nouns, verbs, and modifiers.) An example follows.

Foods	Cooking	Accompaniments
beef	frying	white wine sauce
_____	_____	_____
_____	_____	_____

2. Now list some of the rules which diners obey when making selections (and which are implied by the menu).

Rules

■ Select one element from each category (soup, entree . . .).
■
■
■

3. Here are the selections made by two diners at the restaurant. These are two "texts" created from the system of signs on the menu.

Meal 1	Meal 2
Roman Salad	Chicken soup
Cannelloni	Garlic prawns
Fresh fruits	Fillet steak with vegetables
White wine	Black forest gateau
	Wines
	Coffee

Answer these questions about the texts:

Which is	Number
the least expensive meal?	
the largest meal?	
the most conventional meal?	
the healthiest meal?	

4. Each meal may have a number of possible meanings. Meal 1 may signify "restraint" or "tastefulness" or "poverty."

   Which of the following are *possible* readings of meal 2? (Place a check by your choices.)

   ☐ greediness   ☐ hardship   ☐ independence
   ☐ wealth   ☐ appreciation of good food   ☐ conventionality
   ☐ obedience to custom ☐ experimentation

Different readings of the same text might be produced by people with different interests. For example, which "text" might be favored by:

- the restaurant owner? Why?
- an animal rights campaigner? Why?
- a diner who believed in getting value for money? Why?
- the diner who was paying the bill? Why?
- a cattle farmer? Why?

5. Meanings can be difficult to pin down because the text "itself" does not "contain" or express a meaning. Instead meaning is shaped by:

- the elements selected (properties of the text);
- complex social circumstances (the context);
- the rules applied in reading (reading practices).

6. Any literary text is also constructed from a "menu." What elements and rules might make up the literary menu, or system?

- conventions of narrative;   - _____
- _____   - _____
- _____   - _____
- _____   - _____

What are some texts which can be produced from the system?

- sonnet;   - _____
- lyric;   - _____
- novel;   - _____

What factors shape the meaning given to a specific text?

- its relation to other texts;   - _____
- _____   - _____

Summary

A *text* is a specific object or event constructed from the signs and codes of a social system of meaning.

See also: code
convention
intertextuality
reading practice

Text

Theme

To get you thinking

■ Here is a fable told by Aesop, who lived in ancient Greece.

A hungry wolf was lurking near a flock of sheep, but the vigilant Shepherd gave him no opportunity to satisfy his appetite. One day the wolf came across a discarded sheepskin. He clothed himself in the skin, and so was able to hide among the sheep. This disguise fooled the Shepherd completely, and that night the wolf was herded into the fold with the sheep. But this was the night that the Shepherd chose one sheep from the flock to feed his hungry family. Reaching at random into the pen, the Shepherd picked out the wolf and cut his throat.

■ Does this fable seem to explore some general feature of human existence? If so, what is its subject: deceit? the unfairness of life? greed?
■ To what extent is the meaning shaped by the text itself? To what extent is the meaning shaped by your beliefs and actions as reader?

Theory

In traditional approaches to literature, *theme* refers to the central idea or ideas explored in a literary work. If we use the term in this way we can speak of the theme of generosity in *A Christmas Carol*, or the theme of exploitation in *Heart of Darkness*, and so on. In each case we are assuming that the text has been designed to explore some aspect of human existence.

But this usage assumes that the meaning of a literary work is somehow locked inside, waiting to be released. Modern approaches to literature suggest instead that the meaning of a text is produced by the interaction between features in the text and the beliefs and practices of the people who read it. We must therefore revise the traditional definition of theme to take these "reading practices" into account. In modern usage, then, theme refers to the *major issues or subjects* which become prominent in the *reading* of a text.

Reading practices construct themes by emphasizing or privileging some elements in the text over others, and by applying certain rules (such as "generalizing" the specific elements). The story of "Little Red Riding Hood," for example, can give rise to a range of themes, including:

■ the social oppression of women;
■ the danger of "outsiders";
■ the importance of obedience.

Ways of reading that emphasize the sex of the characters in the story (that is, which privilege *gender*), might focus on the first of these themes. Those which emphasize the social relationships between the characters might focus on the second theme, and so on. These different themes are not all contained "in" the text; they are produced in the process of reading.

Finally, we can make a distinction between theme and *motif*. A motif is an element which we find repeated by a text, or which may be common to many texts. For example, the "wicked stepmother" figure in fairytales, the "quest" formula in adventure tales, or the motorcycle as a symbol of freedom in American movies. Unlike theme, a motif is a feature of the text itself, though it may be open to different readings.

Practice

This well-known poem was written by Percy Bysshe Shelley. Read it through a number of times.

Ozymandias

I met a traveller from an antique land
Who said: Two vast and trunkless legs of stone
Stand in the desert . . . Near them, on the sand,
Half sunk, a shattered visage lies, whose frown,
And wrinkled lip, and sneer of cold command,
Tell that its sculptor well those passions read
Which yet survive, stamped on these lifeless things,
The hand that mocked them and the heart that fed:
And on the pedestal these words appear:
"My name is Ozymandias, king of kings:
Look on my works, ye Mighty, and despair!"
Nothing beside remains. Round the decay
Of that colossal wreck, boundless and bare
The lone and level sands stretch far away.

A number of themes can be invoked through readings of this poem. These could include:

    a. the power of nature;
    b. the foolishness of pride;
    c. the hollowness of male ambition;
    d. the relationship between humanity and god.

1. Ways of reading often relate to different belief systems. Match these belief systems to the thematic readings, a to d above.

Belief System	Theme
Feminism	
Christianity	
Environmentalism	
Pacifism	

2. These thematic readings can be supported by different reading practices, which emphasize different words and phrases in the text. For example: a Christian "allegorical" reading practice might focus on the line "king of kings," which is a title often given to Jesus Christ. Read in this way, the poem can be read as a story about what happened to a ruler who gave himself a title normally reserved for the Christian god. In such a reading, the theme of the poem becomes an exploration of the relationship between human beings and God.

Which features in the poem would be emphasised in the other readings of theme? What rules of reading would be applied?

Theme	Words Emphasized	Rules of Reading
a.		
b.		
c.		
d.	"king of kings"	Look for Christian references

3. The poem begins by using the motif of the traveler's tale. Do you know of any other texts which make use of this technique?

Summary

Theme refers to the central meaning or message which readers attribute to a text. Because themes are produced through the process of reading, different groups of readers may attribute very different themes to the same text, depending upon the beliefs and practices which shape their reading.

See also: reading practices

Theme

Writing and Speech

To get you thinking

■ Here are the opening passages of three stories. Read them; then think carefully about the questions which follow.

The other day I saw a wedding . . . but no! Better I tell you about the Christmas tree. The wedding was nice; I enjoyed it very much, but the other thing that happened was better.

(Fyodor Dostoyevsky, "A Christmas Tree and a Wedding")

Friday A.M. things okay here and hope you are the same. Two details new on the back bar since you enlisted AF. Card Room and Lodge Room per the usual. BOOTS on duty. Well, I was a Sergeant in the last one: *do what they tell you* and—Crown, water-back and the same to you Boots.

(James B. Hall, "Letters Never Mailed")

First there is a red spot, bright, shiny but dark, shading to almost black. It forms an irregular, clearly outlined rosette, extended on several sides by wide streaks of varying lengths which then divide and dwindle until they are no more than meandering threads.

(Alain Robbe-Grillet, "The Secret Room")

■ Which of these three texts is easiest to read? Why?
■ Which text is most likely to provoke argument about its meaning? Why?
■ Can you imagine a speaker for each of the texts? Who might the speaker be?

Theory

In everyday life, we tend to judge the meanings of spoken language according to the intentions of the people who utter the words. We imagine that the words we speak are under our control, and we are likely to get annoyed when people "twist our words" and make a different meaning out of what we say.

Modern literary theory suggests that we have often applied these same rules to written texts. Western cultures have treated writing just like talking, and have assumed that the meanings of written texts should be explainable in terms of some real or imaginary "speaker." This speaker might be the author, or an imaginary character implied by the text. In other words, spoken language has been used as the model for explaining how written language works.

Many traditional literary concepts have been shaped by the "imaginary speaker" assumption. Examples include concepts such as *narrator*, *point of view*, and *tone*. These terms suggest that readers should make sense of written texts by reading the words on the page as the speech of an imagined storyteller who views events from a particular perspective, and who has an attitude toward the events. Such terms imply that a text is a speech to be listened to and understood rather than a structure to be explored. The "speaker" assumption has therefore shaped the kind of texts our cultures produce, and the available ways of reading them.

As a reaction to this emphasis on speech, some theorists have begun promoting written texts which are harder to read as speech, and which exploit more fully the *possibilities* of writing. They argue that speech-like texts merely support the dominant belief in authority figures and expect readers to sit back and accept the meanings offered to them. In contrast, writing should invite us to read *actively*. Once readers learn to be active meaning-makers, it is argued they will find new ways of reading even conventional texts, and of thinking critically about the views that such texts might support.

Practice

Here are two different texts which deal with a hat blowing in the wind.

1. Once when I was walking by the river the wind lifted my hat from my head and carried it off. I ran after it as it blew toward the river, which flowed fast at that spot. My hat was caught briefly by a small bush, but freed itself as I approached, and blew into the water. I had to tear a dead branch from a small tree to fish the thing out before the current swept it away forever.

2. A man is walking by the river. The wind blows. The man's hat rises from his head. The man runs. Oh no, my hat, my hat. Stop! I've lost it. My favorite hat. Changes in air pressure result from the earth's rotation and from diurnal heating and cooling. This results in the movement of air from one region to another. On Jupiter, the winds blow at a thousand miles per hour. The people do not wear hats. A man ran beside a river. A piece of cloth blew in the wind before him. He saw a tree. A bush grew beside the river. Wettable fabrics absorb water by capillary action, the surface tension of the liquid helping to spread it along the narrow fibres. It's wet it will sink no its floating need something to get it out a stick a branch something.

"Ouch" said the tree, and began silently to weep.

One of these is clearly a more common type of writing than the other, yet we can read both of them.

1. A list of different types of writing follows. Place a "1" next to all the types which feature in the first extract, and a "2" next to those which feature in the second.

Types of Writing	Extract
"realistic" narrative	
fantasy narrative	
"objective"/scientific description	
interior/first-person monologue	
reported speech/thought	
present-tense narrative	
past-tense narrative	

Which text, do you think, makes greater use of the *possibilities* of writing?

2. Which extract can more easily be read as the speech of an imaginary person? Is this an effect produced by the text, by the way you read it, or by a combination of these?

3. Here are some possible ways of reading these texts. Place a check by the methods which seem appropriate to each text.

☐ Reading to gain insight into the author/speaker's life.
☐ Reading to find a theme about "life in general" (for example, our struggle to control the world around us).
☐ Reading as a way of activating our own memories of similar experiences.
☐ Reading for the fun of responding to a text in a variety of ways.
☐ Reading to find the author's intention.

Might all of these methods be applied to *both* texts? If so, why do some seem more appropriate than others?

4. Which way of reading is most useful to an education system that emphasizes the teaching and examination of reading skills? (Which methods can be argued to produce answers which are right or wrong?) Does this suggest why few texts like that of "2" above are included in school courses?

Summary

In modern usage, "writing" refers to the practices of making meanings with written signs rather than with verbal ones. Some theorists argue that writing should offer greater possibilities of meaning than speech, because it need not be related to a particular "speaker."

See also: narrative
point of view

Writing and Speech

Index

Term	Page
allusion	93
alternative discourse	51
alternative reading	139
Author	1
authorization	2
Binary Opposition	4
Character	9
character code	20
Class	15
closed text	161
Code	19
Communication	24
Context	28
Conventions	33
Criticism	36
cultural code	21
Culture and Nature	39
Deconstruction	42
Denotation and Connotation	46
diction	156
Discourse	50
dominant discourse	51
English Criticism	53
Feminist Criticism	57
Figurative Language	61
first-person point of view	111

Foregrounding and Privileging	66
Gaps and Silences	70
Gender	74
Genre	78
hegemony	123
Identification	82
Ideology	85
Imagery	88
institution	119
Intertextuality	92
limited narrator	104
Literature	96
Marxist Criticism	100
metaphor	62
metonym	62
mirroring	127
motif	167
Narrative	103
narrator	111
naturalization	40
New Criticism	106
omniscient narrator	104
open text	161
oppositional discourse	51
patriarchy	57
personification	62
plot	104
plot code	21
Point of View	110
Polysemy	114
Poststructuralism	118
Power	122
preferred reading	139

Psychoanalytic Criticism	126
Race	130
reading convention	34
Reading Practices	134
Readings	138
Representation	142
resistant reading	139
resistant reading practice	135
rhetorical device	156
Semiotics	146
sentence organization	156
simile	62
stereotypes	143
story	104
structural code	21
Structuralism	150
Style	155
suspense code	20
symbol	62
syntax	156
textual convention	34
Text	160
Theme	166
third-person point of view	111
Writing and Speech	170

About the Author

Brian Moon has worked as a secondary school teacher and university lecturer in the areas of English, literature, and media studies. He holds a Ph.D. in English, which was awarded for research into literary reading practices, the main focus of his academic work. Moon currently lectures in English curriculum studies at Edith Cowan University in Perth, Western Australia. He is the author of three books from Chalkface Press: *Studying Literature, Literary Terms: A Practical Glossary,* and *Studying Poetry.*

This book was typeset in AGaramond by Electronic Imaging.
The typefaces used on the cover were Alternate Gothic and Fashion
    Compressed.
The book was printed by Versa Press.